Bill W.

Bill W.

My First 40 Years

INFORMATION & EDUCATIONAL SERVICES

Hazelden
Center City, Minnesota 55012-0176

1-800-328-0094
1-651-213-4590 (Fax)
www.hazelden.org

Library of Congress Cataloging-in-Publication Data

W., Bill.
    Bill W.: my first 40 years/Bill W.
       p. cm.
    Transcribed from an audiotape made by Bill W.
    ISBN 1-56838-373-8
    1. W., Bill. 2. Alcoholics—Biography. 3. Alcoholics Anonymous.
  I. Title: My first forty years. II. Title.

HV5032.W19 A3 2000
362.292'86'092—dc21
[B]
                                       99-087571

Editor's note
Minor editing has been done in accordance with Hazelden editorial
style and grammatical usage.

04 03 02 01 00   6 5 4 3 2 1

Cover design by David Spohn
Interior design by Nora Koch/Gravel Pit Publications
Typesetting by Nora Koch/Gravel Pit Publications

Contents

Foreword

Bill W., Bill Wilson, William Griffith Wilson, was born on November 26, 1895, in the small Vermont town of East Dorset. East Dorset, from its beginning, had a different flavor from the town of Dorset. It was a gritty, blue-collar town. The marble quarry owners lived in Dorset, the workers in East Dorset.

Both of the small Dorset towns are approximately six miles north of the larger city of Manchester. Manchester, to this day, caters to well-to-do vacationers and families with second homes in the area. The Equinox hotel has been in operation since 1769, featuring The British School of Falconry and the Land Rover Driving School. The Orvis Company, a fly-fishing and sporting-goods store established in 1856, is down the road from the Equinox.

Part of Bill Wilson's social heritage was a rowdy band of expert riflemen and woodsmen, the Green Mountain Boys, led by Ethan Allen. In 1775, during the Revolutionary War, this group was recognized and sanctioned as an independent military force by the Continental Army. Their headquarters was in Dorset. Their legacy to the people of Vermont was an unabashedly defiant attitude toward authority. Vermonters have a tendency toward being closed mouth, frugal, stringent in public displays of affection, and republican.

The railroad opened in East Dorset in 1851, and those who stopped over stayed at the Barrows House across from the train station. By the end of the nineteenth century, the Barrows House was renamed the Wilson House and was operated by "the widow Wilson." Her grandson, Bill Wilson, was born in a little room behind the bar. During Prohibition, the inn thrived as a stopping-off place for those who could afford to travel to Canada to drink, as it was halfway between New York and Montreal. In those days, the inn catered to the likes of Charles Lindbergh and Myrna Loy.

Near collapse in 1987, the Wilson House was purchased by Ozzie Lepper, who formed a foundation to restore and preserve it, not as a museum but as a living memorial. Now restored as a bed-and-breakfast inn, the Wilson House has guest rooms and a large room for Twelve Step meeting and seminars. Across the green, in front of the church, is the Griffith House where Bill spent part of his childhood with his maternal grandparents. This house has also been restored with a large library and is open for visitors.

Bill and his wife, Lois, are buried in the East Dorset Cemetery, south of East Dorset, just over a mile from the Wilson house. A well-worn path leads to their resting places, which are marked by simple headstones.

During the fall of 1954, Bill Wilson began dictating his
autobiography. At fifty-nine years old, he realized a
dictation of his story would be "more or less tentative and
experimental." It was Bill's intention "to start in with childhood recollections bearing upon my background and ancestry and the events of that time as they related primarily to
my personality structure and the defects in it, which no
doubt laid the groundwork for my alcoholism." Bill wanted
this verbal record to act as an autobiographical sketch to
help researchers for history books to come.

This autobiographical record of the first forty years of
Bill's life is the backbone of the biography written by Robert
Thomsen, *Bill W.*, first published by Harper and Row in
1975 and reissued by Hazelden in 1999. The first section of
Bill W. is an expanded account of this autobiography.

In Thomsen's "Author's Note," he illustrates how he used
this autobiographical taped account from Bill to write his
"absorbing and deeply moving life story of Bill Wilson,
cofounder of Alcoholics Anonymous":

> It is an act of presumption for any man to write the
> life of another—how can any of us be so sure of
> our own perceptions to say in print "this is what
> so-and-so was really like"? When the subject of a
> biography is a man whose life has had a revolution-
> ary effect on hundreds of thousands of others, that
> presumption may seem a kind of impertinence.
>
> Bill W. told his own story many times; he also

wrote about it. Possibly because of New England
reticence, the emphasis was always on the second
half of his life. He gave few details of his childhood, his youth or the early years of his marriage.
However, it was my privilege—my blessing, if you
will—to have known and worked beside Bill during the last twelve years of his life, when he had
begun to understand that his biography would be
written one day.

Thomsen also believed, along with Bill, that the story of
Bill's early years should be aimed at the general reader.

A typed transcript of this autobiography was given to a
Hazelden representative during a visit with Lois Wilson at
her home in Bedford Hills, New York, in November 1986.
Many historians have also been given copies of this public
domain transcript, as was Thomsen.

Those who read Bill's words in the following account will
find insight to this complex, eccentric man. Those who are
familiar with the writings of Bill Wilson will recognize the
simple and humble cadence as Bill expressed himself. The
story was not told to blame his subsequent alcoholism on
any specific events. Instead, a story emerges which shaped
the character of a great man.

The manuscript that follows abruptly ends in the spring
of 1935, as Bill embarks on a business trip to Akron, Ohio.
We are familiar with his meeting with Robert Holbroook
Smith, M.D., (Dr. Bob) and Dr. Bob's last drink on June 10,

1935, the founding date of Alcoholics Anonymous. Dr. Bob also was raised in Vermont, and perhaps future researchers will glean some meaning from AA's cofounders being Vermonters.

If there were to be a dedication to this book, perhaps a phrase from Bill Wilson's last talk to AA members would be appropriate: "I salute you. And I thank you for your lives."

THIS IS September the first, in the year of our Lord 1954. Ed Bierstadt and I are over at the Hotel Bedford, where we propose to begin the dictation of the story of myself and the story of AA from true recollection only. This recording is more or less tentative and experimental, and it is my purpose to start in with childhood recollections bearing upon my background and ancestry and the events of that time as they related primarily to my personality structure and the defects in it, which no doubt laid the groundwork for my alcoholism. . . .

The purpose of this recording is to get into the record what will amount to a biographical sketch of myself and the unfold[ing] of AA as it has appeared to me. It will serve to brief Ed, who is undertaking the research upon the history to come, and will give him a sort of a backbone from which to branch out. No doubt this preliminary construct of the backbone will lack some vertebrae, some ribs, but we do hope to develop some chunks of meat here and there and at least something tangible enough into which he can get his teeth. In the event of anything happening to me, also, it is a simple precaution by way of recording the main events and ideas which have been forthcoming over the years.

> I have always been very much against a biography of any sort, due to our studied policy of playing the founding of this movement down . . .

Of course I have always been intensely averse to anything autobiographical being done in print. Indeed, I have always been very much against a biography of any sort, due to our studied policy of playing the founding of this movement down, for as people in it know, this is a society which can function peculiarly well without too much sanction from the top. Of course, I realize that someday biographies may be written, and there is no legal means of preventing them. Therefore the early part of this narrative is intended to set the record somewhere near straight, and for this immediate purpose I will just try to hit a few highlights in the sketch to follow.

Well, here goes.

I was born in the Green Mountains of Vermont, alongside of a towering peak called Mount Aeolus. I was raised in the parsonage there, although my parents were not in the business of being clergy. One of my earliest recollections is looking out of the window from my crib just as the sunset developed over the great mountain and becoming very conscious of it for the first time. It is an impression which never left me. Somehow, today when I go there, there is no spot quite like this—the spot where I first saw that mountain; that spot in which I can recall so many of the associations of my childhood; that spot whose ancestry and whose native ruggedness endowed me, I fancy, with both strength and weakness.

My father's name was Gilman Barrows Wilson. The family is supposed to have originated in Scotland, migrated to the north of Ireland, to which [my family] can be traced on that side, and thence to this country, where it split up into a Southern branch, a Midwestern branch, and a New England branch, to which I belong. Never having had any special curiosity about these matters, I've never inquired a great deal about my ancestry, hardly knowing it back of my great-grandfather, who originally settled at Manchester, Vermont, the town, [five miles] below [East Dorset].

On my father's side were other family names, notably Barrows. That was the maiden name of his mother, Helen Barrows. I suppose that was an English name. And on that same side of the family there was a family named Cochran, presumably Irish.

Then on my mother's side—the strain is, I expect, predominantly Welsh, as her name was Griffith, later to figure rather prominently in this narrative—was my grandfather [Gordon Fayette Wilson]. And the Griffiths were among the original pioneers of Danby, Vermont, a hamlet just north of East Dorset, that spot in the Green Mountains where I was born on November 26, 1895.

I was born, to be exact, in a hotel then known as Wilson House. Formerly, I believe, it was the Barrows House, and it had been built almost a hundred years ago at this time by Ira Cochran, sister to my great-grandmother Barrows on my father's side. Later on, my grandmother, after the decease of her husband, William Wilson, ran the hotel, assisted by her growing boys, George and my father, Gilman.

I was born, perhaps rightly, in a room just back of the old bar, and I can remember hearing my old friend Mark Whalon, the postman, tell of the great curiosity that he and other children had as this process was going on, hearing my mother's cries there.

I recall, later on, of going on many times to the hotel and

even recall my great-grandmother Betsy Barrows.

My people always were operators of marble quarries—that is, on the Wilson side—and my father inherited the tradition. And I can remember, as a small boy, seeing him set off in a gig for the so-called north quarry. And it was out of this quarry that many noted memorials (I think the Grant's Tomb, perhaps the New York Public Library) and other buildings here in New York City were fashioned. At any rate, my father was a quarryman.

My mother's father, Gardner Griffith, had taken a small . . . farm after the Civil War, and he had chipped out a precarious living until he got the notion of lumbering and then, importing many French woodchoppers, had begun to aggregate a comfortable competence. When I first knew him though, he had moved from the farm and lived at East Dorset in the first house north of the hotel and across the churchyard from it.

My father's people were very amiable and were noted on all sides for their humanity.

My father's people were very amiable and were noted on all sides for their humanity. They were popular folk. They were easygoing folk. They were tolerant folk. Good-natured, good managers, good organizers. In fact, my father was so much so that, when years later, he went to British Columbia to engage in the marble business, greater numbers of old quarrymen in East Dorset left their families to go way out

5

to live in the wilds of British Columbia just in order to work for the one they called "Billy Wilson." Such would be a brief characterization of that side of the family.

Incidentally, alcoholism ran pretty rife on the Wilson side. My grandfather Wilson was a very serious case of alcoholism, and it no doubt hastened his death, although some years prior to this he had, to everyone's great surprise, hit the sawdust trail, to speak figuratively, at a revival meeting in the Congregational Church and was never known to drink afterward. This caused great consternation, Grandmother used to say, among his erstwhile agnostic and hard-drinking Civil War buddies, who then abounded in the town. I say abounded, but that is hardly the case, for East Dorset was, and still is today, only a hamlet of about fifty houses.

On my grandfather's side there was quite a different strain. As I earlier remarked, the town of Danby was probably settled very early by some of the Griffiths, and all of them were people of extremely high native intelligence. They were lawyers and teachers and judges.

One of them, indeed, turned into a super businessman for those days. My grandfather's cousin Silas began to lumber the mountain as a young man, opposite Danby, later bought huge tracts at tax sales, and before the year 1900 . . . had amassed in this little and small state, almost a million dollars, which was a great fortune in those days.

But the Griffiths, though hard driving and people of immense will, immense valor, and great fortitude, had extreme difficulty in forming close relations with other people. They were capable of great love for their own, and this is certainly a factor in my grandfather's relation to me, but somehow they were not overpopular people. They were always highly respected but scarcely dearly loved.

Well, with these preliminaries as background, I might continue on with a few childhood impressions. The next I can remember after seeing the mountain was the occasion of my fourth birthday, when my mother's sister, Aunt Millie, appeared at Grandpa Griffith's and made me a plate of fudge. I suppose the mountain appealed to that which was spiritual in me, but the plate of fudge touched another chord.

Actually, my recollections are rather dim until about the age of seven. What it was, was that my father took the management of a quarry, the Rutland-Florence operation at Rutland, Vermont, and we moved there, where we lived at 42 Chestnut Avenue. Meanwhile, I forgot to say, a sister was born whose name is Dorothy Brewster Wilson, she being somewhat younger than I.

I had, of course, gone to school in the little two-room schoolhouse at East Dorset—I think I can remember my first day there—but was soon transferred, as we moved to Rutland, to the grade school on Church Street not far from our home. I so well recall how stunned and overcome I was by the large number of children around me, and I began to develop a great shyness and at the same time a certain amount of competitiveness. Even then I had developed the trait of persistence bordering on [willfulness], and that set me off on power drives to accomplish objectives. Because of my shyness and awkwardness I began to work overtime to be a ballplayer.

Even at this early age I manifested an interest in science and got a place in the woodshed for a laboratory.

I remember how horrified my father was, when coming home one night, he found that I had mixed certain acids—I've forgotten which now; I should imagine sulphuric and nitric—to make actual nitroglycerine in the back shed. And when he arrived I was dipping strips of paper in the nitroglycerine and burning them. You can imagine what a sensation this made with a man accustomed as he was, in his quarry business, to the use of dynamite, which is but a pale imitation of the real stuff.

I remember how very gingerly Dad lifted that dish, dug a very large hole, which he wet, and gingerly spread the evil stuff about it, and just as gingerly covered it up.

In those days I had a fine companionship with my dad, who used to play ball with me in the yard every night, and on Sundays we would rent a covered buggy—I don't believe that's exactly the name of it, having a flat top with tassels all around—and drive about in some estate and with a great deal of satisfaction.

My mother, however, was a disciplinarian, and I can remember the agony of hostility and fear that I went through when she administered her first good tanning with the back of a hairbrush. Somehow I never could forget that beating. It made an indelible impression upon me, for I really think that she was angry.

At school I don't think that I made any particularly good records. As was to be the case later on, some of my grades were very good and some were very poor. In sports I alternated between being extremely competitive and elated upon success, to being

> At school I don't think that I made any particularly good records. As was to be the case later on, some of my grades were very good and some were very poor.

very discouraged and timid when in defeat, particularly if that defeat took the shape of a good physical trouncing by some smaller kid than I. Even now I was beginning to get oversize for my age.

Meanwhile, all unbeknown to Dorothy and me, a rift was developing between my mother and my father. Temperamentally, as you may already guess, they were very different people. It is altogether probable that my mother should have been a career person, as indeed later she was to be. I recollect, too, my mother was having what they said were nervous breakdowns, sometimes requiring that she go away for extended periods to the seashore, and on one occasion to the sanitarium.

Though I did not know it, and though my father never became an alcoholic, he was at times a pretty heavy drinker. Like me, he was a person to be pretty much elated by success and, together with some of his marble-quarry friends and their financial backing in New York, would have extended sprees. Though I never knew the details, I think one of those episodes had consequences that greatly affronted my mother and increased the strain between them. I never knew exactly what took place, for since that period in Rutland I have not seen my own father more than a dozen times. He died, by the way, on February fourteenth of this year, 1954.

I've seen a great deal more of my mother, though not as much as most children do of their parents, in the intervening years. But Mother was never especially communicative on intimacies. She was, as I have explained, of that rather dour Griffith stock.

Ed just [asked] the question about my friends of this period and about any other brothers or sisters. As I previously said,

I have a sister, Dorothy, somewhat younger than I am, about three years, now married to an osteopathic physician, Leonard V. Strong, today one of the trustees of our foundation and the person who saw me through a great deal of my alcoholic suffering when that had got to be a lonely business. They are living today in Yonkers [New York].

Years later, my father was to remarry after divorcing my mother, the subject I was just approaching, and by that marriage there was another child, so that I have a half-sister, Helen Wilson, now Helen Wilson Riker. She was born in British Columbia [or] Alberta I believe, and she now lives here in New York and is married to one of our AA members.

Now that Ed brings the subject up, I am trying to think about my very early childhood friends, and it is hardly surprising that I cannot remember having any really intimate friends. Playmates, yes, but quite early, due to my shyness and my awkwardness and the developing inferiority, I don't believe that I ever made intimates. My neurosis was under development, and if anything characterizes the neurotic, it is his inability to form partnerships. I was forever trying to dominate somebody or else was dominated by somebody. As I look back on it, I see that that was almost invariably the case.

I recently went back to East Dorset, where among all my childhood friends there is only one person with whom I ever had a close tie. All of the others today are just acquaintances. That acquaintance is the postman, Mark Whalon, now dying of palsy up there. But he was about ten years older than I and when, in later years, I returned to East Dorset, he was a sort of uncle or father to me, and I think in those years I had a certain dependence upon his superior knowledge of the ways of the world and upon his wonderful charm. And that would about sum up the kind of relations I had with other people.

Well, as I have said, at Rutland a storm was brewing between my mother and my father. It was in this period that she had a serious operation called appendicitis at that time. I remember her being an invalid at home. How she sat by the window breathing through a paper tube to get fresh air. Operations were much more serious things in those days.

And then, not too long after this, I would judge, I was told that my father had gone away on a business trip, and he stayed and didn't return. And I imagine that both Dorothy and I sensed that something was wrong. It wasn't long after his departure that we pulled up, Mother, Dorothy, and I, assisted by Grandfather Griffith, and moved back to East Dorset, Vermont, only twenty-five miles away.

The next episode was a shock which I can never forget.

Shortly after we moved back to East Dorset, mother took Dorothy and me on what we thought was to be a picnic at beautiful North Dorset Pond, now called by city folks Emerald Lake. We sat on the southwest shore under a shade tree, and mother seemed very quiet, and I think [Dorothy and I] both had a sense of foreboding. Then it was that Mother told us that Father had gone for good. To this day I shiver every time I recall that scene on the grass by the lakefront. It was an agonizing experience for one who apparently had the emotional sensitivity that I did. However, I hid the wound and never talked about it with anybody, even my sister, let alone Grandfather and Grandmother Griffith, with whom Dorothy and I now went to live.

. . . I hid the wound and never talked about it with anybody, even my sister, let alone Grandfather and Grandmother Griffith . . .

Mother set about to making a living and embarked upon a career. Grandfather Griffith financed her for the Boston College of Osteopathy, and excepting for brief vacation periods, I saw little of her for the next years. Her homecomings were always something for a great deal of joy and excitement, especially the Christmas ones, but somehow I realize now, there was a sort of barrier between Mother and me which has only in recent years dissolved. I loved Father, but I admired and respected Mother. Probably I was always lacking in the right sort of love for her, as I think she was at times for me.

Mother, like Grandfather Griffith, was a person endowed with a tremendous native mind. Neither of them had been much educated. My grandfather had only gone to common school but had always been a voracious reader. Mother had gone a little further. Before her marriage she had prepared for the teaching profession in the so-called Normal School of Castleton, Vermont. With this equipment she set out for Boston to be an osteopath, and I might say here that she succeeded so well that in the many years that followed, she became one of the very best in her city.

Somewhat later on, after [Mother] embarked on a career, Dorothy, my sister, went to live with her, and it fell to the lot of Grandfather and Grandmother Griffith to bring me up in East Dorset, through the years that were to pass until I went to Norwich University, a military college in the state of Vermont. I remember much more vividly this period in school at East Dorset where, after coming from Rutland, I entered the higher grades.

By this time I was ten or eleven, still growing even more rapidly, still suffering from inferiority about my physical awkwardness, and particularly [suffering] with the wound of my father's and mother's separation and subsequent divorce.

I remember hearing Mother and Grandfather talking about this divorce, how it could be brought about. I remember Mother's covert trip to Bennington, Vermont, to see a fearsome man called Lawyer Barber. Somehow I learned that the divorce was complete. This certainly did something to me which left a very deep mark indeed.

It was during this period that I can see how my willpower and distinction, later to keynote my whole life, was developed. I had many playmates, but I think I regarded all of them as competitors. At everything I must excel.

My grandfather, seeing this tremendous drive in me, thought the thing to do was to encourage it. In this period he egged me on at every possible childhood game and occupation. The marble [quarry] business had fallen off, and we were living in a community composed principally of farmers and their families. My chief companions were farmers' sons and daughters and a few of the children of the villagers. We did everything that country kids used to do forty years ago. I was an ardent fisherman. I trapped. I hunted.

In Vermont there is a great military tradition, and so I was early given firearms. I still have a Remington 25-20 rifle that my grandfather bought me when I was only eleven, along with loading tools for cartridges. I used to load these with black powder by the hundreds. I guess I must have stolen every ounce of lead in East Dorset to pour bullets. I remember shooting by the hour with old Bill Landon, a Civil War veteran and a great character who lived next door.

Unlike my grandfather, who would never talk of the Civil War, old Bill would spin me yarns by the hour.

He had been a sergeant on [General Philip] Sheridan's staff, and he used to tell me how on a charge, a minié ball had struck his musket butt, and it passed through and stuck in the skull just over his eye; how he plucked it out and continued the charge. And old Bill had a drooping eye, a scar, and poor sight to prove all this. Old Bill was one of my heroes, and he was also a crack shot, so we were great pals with respect to folklore and shooting irons.

Then, too, his father-in-law was still alive, dear old Frank Jacobs, the shoemaker, a gentle soul who knew nature as no one else around us did. He encouraged me to make bee boxes to track down honeybees to their stores. He pointed out the flowers and the birds. His shoemaking days were coming to the end, but he actually made me a pair one time. And on another occasion he put a new cover on a baseball, a famous dollar-and-a-quarter ball that I just could not part with. I liked the shoes, but I was disappointed in the cover because that was too loose.

> *. . . Rose Landon, was also a great character. She had a great influence on me, both good and bad.*

Bill's wife, Rose Landon, was also a great character. She had a great influence on me, both good and bad. She had been a great beauty in her day and was possessed of a very remarkable voice, so good that someone in Albany [New York] at one time tried to finance her, with the idea that she might well sing upon the Metropolitan stage. Instead, though, she married old Bill, and they had a large family of children, all a little older than I.

Rose was an opium addict, or morphine, I guess it was. One of my early recollections was going to the drugstore and getting her a large chunk of it.

I remember opening the tinfoil around it, smelling the poppy odor, and seeing the white dust accumulated on something that looked like a chunk of beeswax. This she always kept in her apron, and now and then would take small nibbles. Curiously enough, it never seemed to affect her life very greatly. She was a prodigious worker and the effects of the opiate could only be seen just before bedtime, when she would . . . scare me to death by the peculiar way that her eyes rolled up, so that only the whites were visible as she sat in her chair. I remember years later asking her about the effect of the drug, and she said it never done her no harm except to give her a little constipation. So she was what you might call a moderate drug user.

However, she had a very active imagination, no doubt abetted by the drug, and besides teaching me all the music she could and encouraging me about this and that business, she turned out to be a prodigious gossip. And it was from her that I used to hear a tremendous amount of discussion about my father and my mother, and what led up to the divorce, in her judgment.

She rather took the side of my father against my mother, as I recollect. And it was her talk to me, well intended of course, which no doubt accelerated my feeling of being different from other kids who had their own fathers and mothers.

Quite early I learned to swim and got competitive about it. In fact, this began to be so in all sports. I felt I had to be able to . . . bat like Ty Cobb, walk a tightrope like the folks in the circus, shoot like Buffalo Bill, who I had seen breaking glass balls thrown in the air from horseback at the circus in Rutland, Vermont.

My attempt to make a replica of this performance consisted in taking out a hod of coal and, holding my rifle in one hand and tossing a lump of coal into the air with the other, I would try to break the lumps with the rifle. And got so good that I could do about two out of three, although it was a wonder I didn't kill some of the farmers about, as it was a very high-powered gun.

And so it was throughout the whole warp and woof of my

existence. I had to build the best playhouse of any kid in town.

All during this period my grandfather was really the soul of kindness. He loved me deeply, and I loved him as I have few other people. One of my earliest recollections, dating back to the time before we went to Rutland, was that of sitting on his knee and later at his knee, while he read me books of travel. And then came the *Heidi* books [by Johanna Spyri] and the [Horatio] Alger books, and all kinds of things that kids used to read in that time.

And then my neighbor, Rose Landon, installed a circulating library in the now-deserted cobbler shop of her father, which stood near to and just north of her house. And a buckboard used to come up from Manchester each week, and I began to be a voracious reader myself as quickly as I got the ability, reading anything and everything that came into that library. In fact, I used to sleep very little when on these reading sprees. I would seemingly go to bed after being sent there rather sternly by my grandfather, and then I would wait until I felt that they wouldn't notice the light, light up the old kerosene lamp, place it on the floor, and lay a book alongside and hang off the edge of my bed to read, sometimes all night.

So this was the sort of life I led as a kid, and out of it there began to emerge certain events that can characterize me and my personality and emotional structure with still greater vividness.

BILL W.

I must preface this next episode by telling how very much I like to construct things, to work with tools. Also, indeed, with chemicals. My room, which was part of the half-attic on the west side of my grandfather's house at East Dorset, I had turned into a chemical laboratory, and presently to that I added an adventure in radio.

I believe I had one of the first wireless reception sets in Vermont and finally got so I could receive dots and dashes from the station then . . . in Cape Cod. I studied the Morse code and was greatly chagrined that I never could keep up with fast operators. But all this created quite a sensation in the town and marked me out for distinction, something for which, of course, I increasingly craved, until at last that became an obsession.

I made all sorts of things. Bows and arrows. I made an ice-boat, in which I used to sail up and down icy roads. I made jack jumpers, and skis, and sleds. There was an old shop right next to the house where I worked, a deserted blacksmith shop with a good many tools intact. The old blacksmith had gone to his rest. So I was surrounded by all the means of doing everything that a country kid could wish.

The interludes of work, however, at other people's direction didn't please me so much. My grandfather insisted that I learn how to do farm work, and I remember the sweaty afternoons in the cornfield, later getting in fodder, milking the cows. After milking, going down along the stone wall for woodchucks and squirrels and being terribly chagrined because of a bad shot at a heron on King Spring.

At any rate, my grandfather, who warmly approved all my activities, got in the habit of coming to me with what he thought were impossible projects. He thought I needed still more stimulus. So one day he said to me, "Will"—for that's what he called me—"Will, I've been reading a book on Australia, and it says that the natives down there have something they call boomerangs, which is a weapon that they throw, and if it misses its mark, it turns and returns to the thrower. And, Will," said he very challengingly, "it says in this book that nobody but an Australian can make and throw a boomerang." I remember how my hackles rose when he said that nobody but an Australian could do it. I can remember how I cried out, "Well, I will be the first white man ever to make and throw a boomerang." I suppose at this particular juncture I was eleven or twelve.

Immediately I got out all the books I could lay my hands

My grandfather insisted that I learn how to do farm work, and I remember the sweaty afternoons in the cornfield, later getting in fodder, milking the cows.

on at the public library. I found out all I could about boomerangs. Every other interest was deserted except those damned boomerangs. I worked at all hours in the shop on boomerangs, making models from pictures I saw. When I wasn't working on boomerangs, I was throwing them—and failing to get them to return. The significant part of this episode was that here was a challenge to be an absolutely number-one figure in the world. I would be the first white man to do this, so I thought.

The result was that during this long period of constructing boomerangs, I completely lost interest in everything else. My interest in school went to nothing. No filling of the woodbox. I wasn't interested in playmates, just boomerangs, boomerangs, boomerangs. This went for a period of almost six months and at the end of that time, by getting just the right piece of lumber, which I secured by cutting the head out of my bed (my grandfather didn't care for this so much), I did make a boomerang which could be thrown and which could circle the churchyard, and you'd have to jump to get out of the way of it. I called my grandfather out, threw the boomerang, it nearly cut his head off on the return, and I said, "So there." I remember how ecstatically happy and stimulated I was by this crowning success. I had become a number-one man, at least in my child's mind's way of thinking.

That episode in a sense sets the keynote for my whole career. From then on, it was always number one, number one, number one. I came out of my shyness, I came out of—

seemingly came out of a good deal of my inferiority. And then I began a desperate struggle to become number one.

At about this juncture I was sent off to boarding school, at Burr and Burton Seminary, situated at Manchester, Vermont, a town about five miles distance. I boarded there five days a week, returning to East Dorset weekends.

My first experience there that affected me deeply had to do with baseball. In the primary school, that little two-room school in East Dorset, I had excelled. None of the kids about there were very good. But here I was up against a lot of competition. I was still pretty awkward. And out on the playing field at Burr and Burton, on my very first appearance there, somebody threw a ball at me, and I put up my hands and somehow missed catching it, and it hit me in the head. It knocked me down, and I was immediately surrounded by a concerned crowd of kids. But the moment they saw I wasn't hurt, they all commenced to laugh at my awkwardness, and I remember the terrible spasm of rage that came up in me. And I remember how I jumped up and shook my fist and said, "I'll show you! I'll be captain of your baseball team." And there was another laugh. And then started a most terrific drive on baseball.

If I couldn't get anybody to play with me, I threw a tennis ball up against the side of a building. Or I'd spend hours and hours, indeed my whole weekend, throwing rocks at telephone poles to perfect my arm so that I could become pitcher and captain of that baseball team. To this day my right arm won't straighten out. Apparently I injured the socket and got something very much like ringbone on a horse, which prevents the arm from being fully extended. Nevertheless, I did develop a deadly aim and great speed with a baseball, also a lot of ability to throw curves and spitballs and knuckleballs, which were the rage of the day.

I also developed a very high batting average, and during my high school days I think it ran something over .400. So, in spite of my awkwardness, I became the number-one man on the baseball field—the pitcher (he was the hero in those days) and the best batter, and the captain.

And always, always, when I set my mind on it, I could become the number-one man.

Well then, of course, I entered a very happy period. I was beginning to compensate for my inferiorities. And always, always, when I set my mind on it, I could become the number-one man. I became the fullback and the best punter and dropkicker on the football team. And it was with a good deal of reluctance that I yielded the captaincy to a fellow who was just a little better.

At about this period, my grandfather started to stimulate me once more. One day he said to me, "Will, your Uncle Clarence was a wonderful musician. Why, he could play the Jew's harp, and he could play the harmonica, and he could play the fiddle right away, as soon as he took it up." Uncle Clarence had died of [tuberculosis] years before in Colorado. I'd never seen him, but his old trunk was upstairs in the attic and I knew from my investigations that his fiddle was in it. Saying nothing to Grandfather, I went upstairs and got out the old fiddle.[1]

When I got Uncle Clarence's fiddle out of the trunk, it was a pretty battered affair. Of course, I thought it must be a wonderful instrument because it was something belonging

---

1. Editor's note—At this point in the narrative, as he will do occasionally throughout, Bill stops speaking to change the tape, and then summarizes before resuming his story: "This is record number 2 of a considerable series to be made about my childhood and the sources of my maladjustment, my married life, and the experience of Alcoholics Anonymous down to the present day. This is record 2, and on record 1 I have started with my earliest memories and have brought them down to a point where I am in boarding school at Burr and Burton Seminary in Manchester, Vermont, and had just got the idea in my mind that I had to be number-one man in whatever I

to Uncle Clarence. And Grandfather, whose favorite son [Uncle Clarence] was, talked a great deal about it.

Actually, it was a pretty worthless instrument, but I didn't learn that till later. There was only one string on it, which was a D string. I didn't even know that, so I went to the old melodeon [organ] in the parlor and tuned this one string to C. I had sung a little bit in the glee club of the school and had learned a few notes in the bass clef. And so, tuning this one string to C, I got my sister to play, "Work, for the Night Is Coming," which was as far as she could get with the organ. And then I would saw out the tenor by marking the spots on the string where the notes fell. The tenor, I believe, consists of three notes. That was the beginning.

Then I found an old jig book in the melodeon, which showed in the front of it a chart of a violin fingerboard and which strings were which. And then I went over to the old store where Grandfather's brother, Uncle Morley, sat sphinx-like and bought from him a set of wire strings, such as were then used by country fiddlers. I didn't have a bridge, so I fashioned one out of a chip of hardwood that I think I took off the woodpile. And armed with this and the diagram of the fingerboard and the melodeon to tune by, I finally got the thing in some semblance of playing condition and

undertook. We have disposed on record 1 of the boomerang story and my athletic ambitions, and we were just embarking on the subject of music. Burr and Burton Seminary was an old country seminary, co-ed, and a lovely place to be."

pasted the life-size diagram of the fingerboard from the jig book onto the board itself and very laboriously began to saw away.

I announced forthwith that I was going to be the leader of the Burr and Burton Seminary orchestra, which was quite an assignment. In fact, it was only a little time before this that I had been told that I had no ear for music whatever. In fact, my grandfather had strongly intimated it. Then, too, there was the catcher on the ball team. He was very fair-haired and popular among the girls and had a nice tenor voice. I remember being on a ball trip and when I tried to sing, he said, "Shut up, Bill, you've got no ear for music." So that was fuel for the conflagration that was to come.

After he told me this, I went, by the way, to the wife of the principal, who was an Italian, a beautiful person who had once sung at La Scala in Milan. I told [her] that I would like to take music lessons. She afterward informed me that my ear for pitch was so bad that she almost gave it up, but I caught on and, as I said, I did sing very briefly in the glee club and sang just one recital with my friend of the tenor voice. At that point my interest in singing collapsed.

But the fiddle was a real challenge, and to be the leader of the orchestra was a still greater one. That was another one of those number-one power drives.

Well, I delineated the start I made. This was followed up by spending hours listening to the victorola, which had just put in an appearance. And I began to hear [violin] artists like

. . . [Mischa] Elman and [Fritz] Kreisler, and then I would go back to my room in the seminary and caterwaul on those strings, and spent all my weekends at home on it. Meanwhile, all other interests go, as in the case of the boomerang. No athletic practice, studies neglected. I just had to learn to play that goddamned fiddle. I got exercise books. I got other books illustrating the proper positions for bowing and fingering. I began to play scales and arpeggios and exercises. And at the end of two years' time I did play first violin in the high school orchestra, which was a very bad first violin and it was a very poor orchestra, but I did do it.

. . . I did play first violin in the high school orchestra, which was a very bad first violin and it was a very poor orchestra . . .

Well, that made me another number one. In this period my happiness was very great, because on all fronts I was succeeding. In my studies, things were very spotty. Where the interest was high, my marks would go from 95 to 98, such as in chemistry and physical geography and astronomy.

Curiously enough, I never had good marks in English and often flunked the courses and would have to take them over. The same was true of language. In geometry I was exceptionally good, but I never in the world could learn algebra. However, I was getting by, and I also began to be number one in other respects. For some reason or other, I was made president of the YMCA.

At this juncture, despite my homely face and awkward figure, one of the girls at the seminary took an interest in me. [The girls] had been very slow to do that when I first appeared and I had a terrific inferiority respecting the gals. But now comes the minister's daughter, and I suddenly find myself ecstatically in love.

Now, then, in this discussion to come I'm going to make quite a point of an easily understood triad of primary instincts which result in primary drives. The drive for distinction and power; the drive for security—physical, financial and emotional; and the desire to love and be loved, romantically or otherwise.

Well, you see, at this period, now that I am in love, I am fully compensated on all these primary instinctual drives. I have all the prestige there is to have in school. I excel, indeed I'm the number one where I choose to be. Consequently, I am emotionally secure. My grandfather is my protector and is generous with my spending money. And now I love and am loved, fully and completely for the first time in my life. Therefore, I am deliriously happy and am a success according to my own specifications.

Now comes an episode which had a profound bearing on the later years. One morning the principal of the school came in, and at chapel he announced with a very grave face that Bertha Banford, the minister's daughter and my beloved, had died suddenly and unexpectedly the night before.

I recently revisited that chapel, where there is a plaque commemorating that girl. She made such a profound influence on everyone. There is only one other plaque of its sort in the chapel in all these years. And looking at it I could still feel the terrible blow on that morning. With me it was simply a cataclysm of such anguish as I've since had but two or three times. It eventuated in what was called an old-fashioned nervous breakdown, which meant, I now realize, a tremendous depression. Interest in everything except the fiddle collapsed. No athletics, no schoolwork done, no attention to anyone, wanted to be alone, utterly and deeply and compulsively miserable. I used to sneak out and go to the graveyard where she was buried, and my whole career and my whole life utterly collapsed.

At this time I couldn't be a number-one man. I couldn't be anybody at all. I couldn't win, because the adversary was death, and at that time I didn't know there wasn't any death. So my life, I thought, had ended right then and there.

I got askew of the faculty. My German teacher rated me at 40. For that reason I didn't graduate. My mother came up, terribly angry, from Boston. A stormy scene from the principal. Here I was, president of my class by this time, senior class, and I can't graduate. So the end had come. I don't know how I ever got through the next summer. It was spent in utter empathy, often running into anguish, in compulsive reflection, all centering around the minister's daughter.

Somehow that summer, though, I did complete the course in German, and my mother hustled me down to live with her at Arlington, just outside of Boston, where she'd taken a house and where she'd brought my sister and a couple of friends. I was entered in the Arlington High School and barely got through some courses there. The idea of this was to prepare me for the examinations for the Massachusetts Institute of Technology. Because of my scientific interests it was supposed that I should be an engineer. I took the examinations and could hardly pass a one of them.

Somehow or other I was entered into Norwich University, the military college of the state of Vermont, where the entrance requirements were easy and I could be certified from the seminary without examination.

So I entered Norwich University. Meanwhile, I had made

the acquaintance of the wonderful person to whom I am now married. She was then Lois Burnham, daughter of a Brooklyn physician who brought his family to North Dorset, Vermont, where they occupied a cottage which stands on the very spot [on which] Mother had told me of her impending breakup with Father. I think Lois came along and picked me up as tenderly as a mother does a child. I was attracted to her. I began to fall in love with her. However, that was a summertime affair and, as I say, I soon entered Norwich University Military College, where the discipline was quite as strict as at West Point.

Again I felt I was nobody. I couldn't even begin to compete in athletics, in music, or even for popularity with the people around me. I so keenly remember when the rush for the fraternities was on and I didn't get a bid to a single one. I

> . . . Lois came along and picked me up as tenderly as a mother does a child.

remember how I tried out for baseball and football and wasn't good enough for either first team. I remember how there was a fellow who played the violin so much better than I that I couldn't even get into the dance orchestra. I remember how I produced an old cello that I had and somehow scraped up a part in the glee club with that. But I was very second-rate. Some of my studies I handled very well, others I began to fail in.

Suddenly came a hazing incident that took all our class

out of school for a time. When I returned, this was a great relief to me. Then I returned with fear and trembling. By this time I got a bid from one fraternity and turned it down. I lived more and more to myself, although God knows I had some lively company about me.

My roommate was a man who became a considerable author. His name was Leonard H. Nason, and he wrote *Chevrons*, one of the best accounts of [World War I]. And he was a kid absolutely full of spirit and mischief. By contrast I realize how very depressed and lone wolf I was.

Running one day for class, I slipped on the ice and, putting down my hand, knocked my elbow out of joint, the one that was already crooked from so much baseball pitching. It was a very simple matter to put it in joint, but significantly, I absolutely insisted on going all the way to Boston to let my mother, then an osteopathic physician down there, look after it. Mother marveled that I hadn't had the thing reduced at school, but she of course got the job done. At the same time, I think I raked out some adenoids and tried to straighten the elbow. At any rate it was a harmless set of jobs and I remember starting for the train, how terribly reluctant I was to face that discipline and that idea of being no good and second-rate.

As I got on the train going from Boston back to Northfield, [Vermont,] I began to have terrible sensations in the solar plexus. I felt like the world was coming to an end.

Oh, in this period Lois had gone back to Brooklyn. They

went there in the wintertimes. I had just met her there, I think, the summer before and the acquaintance had just started. At any rate, the sensation that I was going [to] die increased. I began to be seized with terrible shortness of breath and frightful palpitations. It seemed as though I just couldn't get air enough. And to the surprise of the conductor I left the coach and eventually lay down in the vestibule, with my nose to a crack in the floor to see if I couldn't get air. I was just in stark panic that I had heart trouble and was going to die. That I'd got heart trouble and was going to die thereafter became an absolute fixation.

Somehow I struggled back to school, but the minute I'd be called for reveille in the morning and asked to do a few simple exercises, this terrible palpitation would set in once more and I'd collapse. Of course, I was promptly taken to the infirmary, and absolutely nothing was the matter with me. And yet I was just overcome with this obsession. And it would result in actual and very heavy palpitations. So, at the end of a couple of weeks I was sent back to my grandfather, which was just where I wanted to go.

Well, arrived in East Dorset, I was rendered really immobile. I could do nothing. I used to go into fits of palpitation and cry to have the doctor brought, who would give me some bromide and tell me to buck up and try to persuade me there was nothing the matter with my heart.

Well, it takes very little psychiatry knowledge to figure that situation out. I wanted to die and my heart was broken and there wasn't any use going on, that was the unconscious complex, beyond any doubt.

Well, summer came and Lois appeared, and she lifted me out of this despond and we fell very deeply in love. And I was cured temporarily of my neurosis, which is to say that I had made a fresh compensation, because now I loved and was loved and there was hope again. Still, I remember long conversations with her in which I declared myself to be no good, couldn't face school again, couldn't bear leaving her. At the unconscious level, I have no doubt she was already becoming my mother, and I haven't any question that that was a very heavy component in her interest in me.

Lois was the daughter of a very dominating father, and she was four and a half years older than I. Moreover, she represented areas in which I had always felt a great inferiority. Her people were of a fine family in Brooklyn. They were what we Vermonters called "city folks." She had social graces of which I knew nothing. People still ate with their knives around me, the back doorstep was still a lavatory. So, her encouragement of me and her interest in me did a tremendous amount to buck me up.

But back to school I had to go. Well, at the school there occurred one terrific effort to compensate. I was failing miserably in calculus, which of course, is built around and is a tremendous extension of algebra, and was a mathematical invention, one of the great triumphs of the mathematical mind.

Well, calculus as students learn it is really just a set of formulas. And being confronted with problems, they are taught which formula to apply, and the solution falls out forthwith. Well, as I have said before, I always had great difficulty with algebra and [calculus] required the memorizing of a lot of formulas, and I couldn't memorize them. I realized that I was going to be an absolute flat failure in calculus. In fact, the professor promised me that I would get zero.

As I just remarked, the basis of calculus rests in a tremendous mathematical invention. Leibniz and Newton both arrived at this advanced thinking and concept together. And the underlying theory and grasp of this thing is really a great abstraction, and not a very easy one to lay hold of. And I began to sense after I had plied the professor with questions, that he really had not laid hold in a deep sense of the underlying principal of the whole damn business. He was a catalog of formulas, he could apply the formulas, he was glib, but deep down he didn't know how the goddamned thing worked. And I made up my mind I would learn.

So I went over to the library and I read the history of mathematics and all that led up to the evolution of the concept of calculus, and finally, for a brief few days, I did lay ahold of the concept so that I knew it. By this time I had developed considerable talent in argument, and I got the professor over a barrel and I made a fool out of him before his class, and he did give me zero, but I had won one battle. In other words, I was the only one on the school grounds, the number-one man again, the only one who deeply understood the underlying principles of calculus.

He was a catalog of formulas, he could apply the formulas, he was glib, but deep down he didn't know how the goddamned thing worked.

Well, I was saved from nongraduation by the outbreak of World War I. By this time I had begun to be far more popular with my schoolmates. I was in my third year at Norwich, but actually only a sophomore because of the interruption of the course due to the hazing incident, on which the whole class was expelled because no one would tell. I had become very much more popular and had begun to relate myself better to people, and I believe I had been given a little authority. I had been made a corporal or a sergeant in the corps, and then it was discovered that I had talent for instructing people. Curiously enough, though awkward myself, I had talent for drilling people. I had a voice and I had a manner that would compel a willing obedience and so much so that the attention of the commandant was drawn to it.

Then, suddenly, the globe exploded into World War [I], and I am projected into Plattsburgh. Meanwhile, I had been seeing a great deal more of Lois and by this time we were engaged.

Well, [in May 1917] I arrived at Plattsburgh with the first contingent and in the first camp.[2]

My feelings were certainly mixed. In Vermont there is a tremendous military tradition. The part of the citizen was to willingly, gladly, joyously bear arms. I would get that from my grandfather and I especially got it from old Bill Landon, the Civil War vet. If your country needed you, you were supposed to go and not even think of asking any questions. One of the worst forms of opprobrium that could be cast on anybody when I was a kid was to be called a "slacker." Those who failed to go to the Civil War, evaded service, or got some sort of an easy job got a stigma that they carried all their lives.

I can remember old John Bee, a wealthy and respected citizen of our town—that is respected in some quarters—who

2. Editor's note—Bill stops his narrative here to change tapes. He then briefly summarizes prior to resuming: "This is side 2 of record 2. I had just arrived at Plattsburg, and if memory serves me correctly, it was May 1917."

nevertheless had this stigma on him. Old Rose Landon, my friend of next door, used to tell me how all during the Civil War, John was ill and used to toddle down to the village with a long shawl over his shoulders, very much stooped, with a bottle of smelling salts, and how all during that period no one would speak to him.

Nothing, either, was worse than a Copperhead [a Northerner who supported the South during the Civil War]. And when I was a kid, the Copperhead and the Democrat of Vermont were about of the same breed.

So I had this terrific sense of patriotism. I had this terrific sense of freedom, which goes to a length among Vermont people that the nation scarcely understands. And here I was, approaching Plattsburgh.

Well, neurotic that I was, I was ambivalent. The great upwellings of patriotism would overtake me one day, and the next day I would just be funked and scared to death. And I think that the thing that scared me most was that I might never live my life out with Lois, with whom I was in love.

However, things began to move pretty well in Plattsburgh at first. Because of the strenuous two years of virtual West Point discipline, we of Norwich had a tremendous head start on the rest of the camp and stood out miles above average. Besides, as I have said, I had begun to develop some flair for leadership, so I got on very fast and very well with the instruction. And I liked it too and yet, underneath was this ghastly fear. Maybe my number was up and now I wanted to live, because I loved and I was loved, and in this environment I was again sure of myself.

Then a decision was put up to us in Plattsburgh in that first camp. We could have a choice of our branch of service. Should we become aviators and fly those creaky crates in combat? Should we become infantrymen? Should we join the quartermaster corps? Should we be field artillery men? Or should we be coast artillery men?

Well, that choice, when put up to me, threw me into a fresh agony and finally, despite all the great tradition of my state and of my school, I chose the coast artillery. The only mitigating circumstance was that the coast artillery was to be the training ground for the larger pieces which would be used for large mobile artillery which would be used abroad. However, I figured it

. . . I had begun to develop some flair for leadership, so I got on very fast and very well with the instruction.

would take a long time to train and beside, the eight-inch howitzer[s] operate a long ways behind the lines, it would be safer.

So I put my money on safety, and I was overwhelmed immediately with my first great dose of guilt and shame. Well, those of us who made that choice (most of them were engineers and technical experts, and people who also wanted to be safe) were shipped one evening just after mess to Fort Monroe, Virginia, and as the train pulled out, a half of the Plattsburgh camp stood around us and jeered, "Playing it safe!" I never had, at least for many years, such a terrible feeling of shame and guilt. How I had let my ancestors down! How none of those who came across the mountains with rifles and axes would have acted like that!

Well, I finally arrived at Fort Monroe and immediately found myself up against technical studies that were very difficult. I had to brush up on math. Some of the courses I liked very much, but we were driven at a stupendous pace, the weather was desperately hot, so I would alternate between periods of real enjoyment and outbursts of patriotism, because I learned that we were training to go abroad, and again this fear. Then Lois would come to see me and my fear to go abroad would be redoubled.

Finally, the course was completed and I was commissioned as an artillery officer at just twenty-one. Actually I had entered Plattsburgh, I think, slightly underage. Well, I got a tremendous bang out of being commissioned, and we were given a little time off, and there was a wonderful interlude on the lake at North Dorset, and with Grandfather at home, and then notice of my station camp. I was to continue training at Fort Rodman, Massachusetts, which lies on a point just outside of New Bedford. So, presently I arrived there with new uniform and gear, find myself on an old Army post and among three kinds of troops: drafted men, volunteers, and regular-army folks. On the post were a number of old, seasoned regular officers and some noncommissioned officers of the old army.

The post, up to the time we arrived, was going on exactly as it had for perhaps forty years. It was utterly intact. All of the atmosphere and tradition of the old army was there.

Well, I enjoyed that, too, and, of course, I was put in command of men. I was very encouraged to see the effect that I had on them and began to gain confidence, but still there was this undertone of fear about going abroad.

Meanwhile, the society people in town began to invite the young officers to their homes. One of the great fortunes and one of the leading families of New Bedford was the Grinnell family. Cotton mills, sprinkler systems, and so on. And they were very rich and very much socialites. I remember so well Emmy and Catherine Grinnell. Emmy's husband had gone off to the wars, Katy had lost hers, and the two of them used to entertain a group of us kids at their house. This was the first time in my life that I had ever seen a butler. This was the first time in my life that I had ever been out in society. And a great rush of fear and ineptitude, self-consciousness swept over me. In conversation I could hardly say two words. The dinner table was just a terrible trial.

And then somebody put into my hands a Bronx cocktail [gin, dry and sweet vermouth, and orange juice], my very first drink. All during college I had backed away from drinking. I'd been told how many of my ancestors went down with it. I used to look down, too, upon those boys, such as my roommate, who would go to Montpelier and drink beer and perhaps naughtily consort with blondes. That was very much beneath me. Besides, I was frightened of liquor. But here it was.

Well, my self-consciousness was such that I simply had to take that drink. So I took it, and another one, and then, lo, the miracle! That strange barrier that had existed between me and all men and women, even the closest, seemed to instantly go down. I felt that I belonged where I was, I belonged to life, I belonged to the universe, I was a part of things at last. Oh, the magic of those first three or four drinks! I became the life of the party. I actually could please the guests. I could talk freely, volubly. I could talk well. I became suddenly very attracted to these people and fell into a whole series of dates.

But I think even that first evening, I got thoroughly drunk and within the next time or two, I passed out completely, but as everybody drank hard, nothing too much was made of that.

> Oh, the magic of those first three or four drinks! I became the life of the party.

Meanwhile, as I have said, Lois and I were engaged. She came over to see me. I was rather reluctant to introduce her to my new friends. After all, they didn't frown on liquor in the Burnham household, but they weren't going at this rate. So I felt very awkward. Nevertheless, they invited her to one of the parties, and I kept the lid on my drinking and again felt very, very much on the inferior side. I think it was on that visit that we decided that we'd be married before I went abroad, and I remember coming to Brooklyn once more.

Well, I came back there, this time to be married to Lois and again, without liquor, I felt the old awkwardness and inferiority, although her father and mother and most of her friends went out of their way to make me feel comfortable. I guess there were some, at least so I think, who said, "Where did Lois get that one?" At any rate, we were married [in January 1918], and we returned to New Bedford and we got commutation, so we got an apartment downtown, and I only had to get to the post in time for reveille.

That was a pretty ecstatic period. We had parties ourselves, we served liquor, and Lois at once began to get concerned, because about every third party I'd manage to pass out entirely. But then, it was a glad, bad time and a very happy one on the whole, marred however, by this nagging undercurrent of "When shall we sail?" Down deep I was still scared and very, very ashamed.

In the spring or early summer of 1918, sudden orders came for a move to Newport, Rhode Island, where regiments were being assembled at Fort Adams. We had trained, meanwhile, on the old coast pieces, continued our course on ballistics and, I think, had learned something of the eight-inch howitzers to which we were later to be assigned. At any rate, we land in Newport, and this time I have to live in a tent on a part of the old parade ground, whilst Lois and the wives of the other officers congregated in Newport itself.

We could see each other perhaps an evening a week and on the weekends. The parting was coming closer, and we knew it.

Finally, the dreaded day arrived. I remember going with an officer called McConnell and his wife, the four of us, to someplace down on the shore for lobster. I remember the tremendous pall of gloom that settled over three of us, all save Lois, who bore up. Then I remember getting a terrible aversion to that mood of pessimism and thought how very selfish and self-concerned this all is. And afterward, Lois and I got away from them, and at sunset time we stood on one of the beautiful cliffs at Newport overlooking the sea. It was a part of the shoreline where [we] were utterly alone, she and I, looking out over the ocean, wondering. The sun was just setting. And as the minutes passed our gloom was superseded by a growing feeling of duty and patriotism, and we talked about those things, and then it turned into an exaltation that I now realize amounted to a genuine spiritual experience. In other words, we found exaltation in the joy of sacrifice. We were given the strength and the joy to go on in the face of utter perilousness over the circumstances. That was the first outline and trace of the spiritual experience mechanism as it evolved in me over the years. I never shall forget that experience. It was very triumphant.

So, when we marched away and were loaded on the train, and I waved to Lois out of the car window as we pulled out for Boston, it wasn't too bad. In fact, it was very good. Then on shipboard, we moved out of Boston harbor in the night, and the next day we had a rumor that there had been some shelling of barges off Cape Cod, presumably by German submarines. And that sent a chill up my spine, but I was delighted to find that it wasn't a chill of fright.

We came into New York harbor, after circling around, picked up some more troops, and then the good old British ship *Lancashire* set sail toward the east.

Well, I'll never forget that voyage. There were a lot of nurses on board, we soon got next to the steward, I got hold of one of the ship's officers and struck up a comradeship with him. He gave me my first experience with brandy, which was so elevating that I can understand why Mr. Churchill drinks it.

There was some undercurrent of apprehension, but the ship's company was really full of joy and confidence. There was anxiety, but somehow you could move that aside.

Then came an experience that was a tremendously releasing and assuring thing for me. We had moved up almost in sight of Iceland, and it got terribly cold. We knew we might be there, as we afterward learned we were. And then finally we took our turn to the southeast and entered the Irish Sea, which at that time was absolutely infested with German submarines. We all realized we were entering the sea presently, but still I didn't feel too concerned, nor did I see anyone else who betrayed any apprehension.

At this time we had to set most rigorous watches. Stairwells had been built down the hatches of the *Lancashire*, and there were openings from the stairway into one deck after another, and those decks were just packed solid with bunks. So they put an officer at each landing on the stairway in the hatch opposite each deck filled with bunks, so that if during the night we were hit, we'd be there to handle things and stop any panic. And I had an early-morning watch on the night the *Lancashire* came into the Irish Sea.

I sat practically on the keel of the vessel, and I could look up the stairway, and through the hatch I could see daylight just coming. I

. . . it reminded me of the time I stuck my head inside the old church bell, and a kid pounded the bell with a rock.

couldn't help but reflect that I was the man lowest down, and I was musing away when suddenly there was an ear-shattering crash. Thinking about it afterward, it reminded me of the time I stuck my head inside the old church bell, and a kid pounded the bell with a rock. It was utterly shattering, and the ship trembled and shook, and I thought to myself, "This is it." Then a rush from the bunks started. Sleeping men making for the hatchways. And I found I had to offer to shoot them to stop it. And the minute I drew my gun and quieted those people down, although we all thought our number was up and not a chance, another tremendous spiritual experience, this wave of complete confidence and exaltation. The feeling, "Well, you aren't yellow, after all."

Well, as it fell out, what had happened was that a destroyer going along nearby—a torpedo had been fired at us and missed and the destroyer had dropped an ash can, as they called [depth charges], off the stern, in the effort to get the submarine. And it was so close by that the impact of that terrific explosion against the hull gave every feeling that you'd just got hit.

Well, we finally got up on deck and, boy what a day! A little blimp put off from the Scottish coast, which had then come into sight. He comes out and he hovers alongside our bridge. The respective captains exchange their compliments, and this small, one-man blimp, motor-driven, was able to scout around the convoy and spot submarines. They couldn't get very near the surface. And the blimp would come and hang over a submarine, the destroyer rush underneath and drop the ash can. Every time we saw what we thought was a periscope, we'd let the six-inch guns go and, gee, I just enjoyed that. It was getting bad.

So, for me, World War I started very auspiciously. It was then the very height of the submarine menace. England thought she might be starved. The Germans were pushing ever closer to Paris. And that seventy-five-mile long-range gun was beginning to get into action. Things looked pretty dark. But the French held, people got there and were quartered outside of Winchester for a time, and I think we had some sort of a little epidemic in camp that slowed our departure down. We were allowed to go into town all the time. I think this would be about July 1918. Anyway, it was midsummer.[3]

In Winchester, there came another illuminating experience. We were, of course, permitted to sightsee in town, and one of the very first places I visited was old Winchester Cathedral. Before going in, I remember wandering in the graveyard and came across a headstone of someone called Thomas Thacher, perhaps an ancestor of my good friend Ebby [Thacher]. And I remember what a smile I got out of the epitaph. Perhaps I saw it coming out of the cathedral, I guess I did, come to think of it. At any rate, here's the epitaph:

---

3. Editor's note—Bill stops, changes tapes, and summarizes: "This is record 3, side 1. In my narrative, we've been under convoy down the Irish Sea in the last of record 2, and we've now arrived at the town of Winchester, where we were detained on account of an epidemic."

Here lies a Hampshire grenadier
Who caught his death drinking cold small beer.
A good soldier is ne'er forgot,
Whether he dies by musket or by pot.

I spoiled my story; I saw that coming out.

At any rate, I walked inside the cathedral, and there was a company of soldiers there, some of them pretty tough-looking specimens, and all were very much subdued by the atmosphere of that place. I have been in many cathedrals since and have never experienced anything like it. Returning there in 1950, I went through a similar experience. There was within those walls a tremendous sense of presence. I remember standing there and again the . . . spiritual experience repeated itself. I thought of France, I thought of wounds, I thought of suffering, I thought of death, even of oblivion. And then my mood veered sharply about as the atmosphere of the place began to possess me, and I was lifted up into a sort of ecstasy. And though I was not a conscious believer in God at the time—I had no defined belief—yet I somehow had a mighty assurance that things were and would be all right. And then it was that I went out and read the inscription about the Hampshire grenadier, and once more I was possessed with the spirit of adventure, and the spiritual experience. And the depression that had preceded it vanished into the background.

That was very much like the experience at Newport, very much like it, except this time the notion of the supernatural and the notion of God kept crossing my mind, and the sense of some sort of sustaining presence in that place was quite overpowering. I didn't define it, but it was a valid spiritual experience and it had the classic mechanism: collapsed human powerlessness, then God coming to man to lift him up to set him on the high road to his destiny. Those were my impressions of my experience in the cathedral.

Presently we were marching down the twenty miles of road to Southampton, we boarded a transport in the late afternoon. At dark she slipped her cable, and at last we

. . . the notion of God kept crossing my mind . . .

were off to the high adventure. I remember that I actually enjoyed the run across the Channel without lights, the precautions we had to take in the murk lest a cigarette or a match show, the thrill of coming closer to the enemy. And again the apprehension leaked through hardly at all.

Of course, I'd had a wonderful time in England, and out in the country villages and lanes you could see people still dressed and acting like the characters in Dickens. Every now and then the cathedral experience would return.

And here we were alongside a pier in Cherbourg. There I got a shock. There was a large English camp at Cherbourg, which we were to occupy, and one of their officers had come down to expedite all this. And I remember the captain of our battery, a hard-boiled contractor from Milwaukee, and how he'd got his captaincy in spite of the boys from the Massachusetts Institute of Technology, who were so much better in ballistics. But he was a rough-cut diamond, and for the first time I saw English culture and dignity in conflict with American pugnacity and childishness and lack of grace. I remember with shame the awful bawling out that our captain gave this British colonel, who greatly outranked him.

Then I remember being in the streets of Cherbourg, marching toward camp, and I was possessed by Europe, and I loved it at once. And despite my three years' French in school, never having learned to speak a word, I remember straining at the words of these urchins and finally gathered that there was a prison on the hill where there were German prisoners. Yes, we were coming closer.

Then we were on the outskirts, and here [we] were in a camp just occupied by the British. Then I saw the traditions the other way around. The British common soldiers had to sleep in a little circular tent, not more than twelve feet in diameter, with wooden floors, and if you put a dozen men in these, they all had to put their heads out and pile their feet in the middle. Whilst we officers had a tent of our own, another tent with a bath in it, and a valet, and I felt terribly ill at ease and very angry with our British cousins. Those were some of the early impressions.

Then we were shipped south, to [a] town . . . outside of Limoges, where the great chinaware is made. And here I was quartered with a French family, the men all gone to war, the old grandmother taking care of a child of four or five, the wine on every side, which I gobbled up greatly, the very different French attitude toward drinking than ours. I marveled that none got drunk. And I remember one terribly cold morning, crawling out from between those two feather mattresses and coming downstairs, and found the young child of four or five with a few twigs, pointing up to the shelf and lustily crying, "Ca," and he was pointing to a bottle of rum. And finally Grandmother obligingly came along and poured him a good, stiff nip, which he downed. By this time my French was enough to understand that that was to keep illness away from the small boy.

Well, we trained, and about this time promotions began to come around, and again the desire to be a number one had seized me, but my promotion got lost somehow in the mails and it didn't show up. And then we were moved to the artillery range, and this time we were to actually fire our pieces.

It was the tiny village . . . among the mountains, and I remember how our batteries and our battalion were set up, dug into a bank. We were supposed to fire over a low hilltop and into the country beyond. How the pieces were set up, how the MIT men figured firing data, spending two hours to make their calculations, how we carefully measured off the distance between the guns. And I was finally sent out about nine miles away, to the place where the shells would supposedly land. And about three hundred yards from us, off in a field, was set up a hunk of canvas which was merely a pinpoint on the map, on which the four guns to fire were supposed to be trained. And we were in a slit trench with a periscope to observe the operation. When number-one gun was fired, we could hear the report in the phones and we were terrifically thrilled, when down came the shell practically on the mark. Boy, we thought we were good. Then number four was fired and all of a sudden there was a terrible sinking in the solar plexus, a feeling that the earth was opening up in a yawning pit, a frightful sinking sensation and an awful concussion. Tons of dirt were blown all over us and we barely crawled out of that slit trench to find that the number-four gun had forgot to offset against number one, and he was trained right on us. Well, that was my first experience with death close at hand.

And we were [there] when the Armistice was signed. The town went crazy. There I saw my only drunken Frenchman, who embraced me in a dark alley, mumbling about how wonderful these Etats-Unis were, and presently we were sent off to Bordeaux, and after a while we were shipped home, and Lois met me at Hoboken, and life started again.

Well, like all returning vets, I ran into difficulties. I was much surprised, for example, in the New York subways, when the guards failed to salute me and when the passengers pushed me around. And because I had got some sort of shock because of a motorcycle jumping a bank and nearly killing some of us, I found to my horror that I had a hex when we went under the river to Brooklyn.

Then the question was for employment, and Lois's father, who had a good standing in Brooklyn, exerted every influence, but to no avail at all because I hadn't finished college, I really wasn't trained for anything, and I finally wound up just across the street from where our AA office now is—I think it was 466 Lexington—anyhow, the New York Central [Railroad] office building. And there I went to work as a clerk in the

I was much surprised, for example, in the New York subways, when the guards failed to salute me and when the passengers pushed me around.

insurance department. In fact, I worked for my brother-in-law, Cy Jones, who was at that time the head clerk.

Well, it was [a] tremendous comedown from being an officer and awfully, awfully hard to take, especially from a brother-in-law. I worked there some months and turned out to be such a very bad bookkeeper and manager that the New York Central fired me. And that produced a mighty rebellion in me that I would show this town and that I would show these socialite friends of Lois's. In fact, I would show the whole goddamned world.

At that time the socialist plum plan for taking over the railroads was involved, and very briefly, despite my Vermont training and origin, I turned quite socialist—a reaction, I expect, against the New York Central.

And then again started the quest for a job, and I had a period of flunking and slumping. Finally I took a job up on one of the New York Central piers, driving spikes in planks after the carpenters had sawed them off and laid them down, and that got me up very early in the morning way over in Brooklyn, and I had to work up around Seventy-second Street, and I ran into the New York unions.

Well, I wasn't so socialistic now. I objected very much to joining the unions, and I was threatened by force, and I left the job rather than to join the unions. And meanwhile, the drinking had been crawling up. And all during army life I had done all the drinking possible, but was never drunk on duty. During the long wait at Bordeaux, I used to have a bottle of rum and, I think, it was a bottle of sherry, under my bed, which happened to be in a chateau, and each morning the gatekeeper's wife would come in with a great big bowl of steaming coffee, and she would get the rum bottle out from under the bed and hold it over until I said, "Halt!" And I would so be fortified for reveille, and drank nearly all day but got into no trouble.

Now, here in New York, the family didn't approve of regular drinking, and so I turned more to episodes, which began to be worrisome again. Nevertheless, a tremendous drive for success was on. But, meanwhile, partly as an escape, partly because we wanted to get together, partly because we wanted to think, Lois and I determined upon a walking trip. We went to Boston, took a boat to Portland, Maine, and walked, carrying packs and army pup tents, in which we lived, from Portland, Maine, over to Rutland, Vermont. And that was a very happy, joyous experience which postponed getting busy to show the world.

Well, when we returned to New York, we couldn't live forever with Lois's father, Dr. Burnham, and her very wonderful mother. By this time Lois had reentered occupational therapy, something for which she was very well paid during the war. She was bringing in a little money, but what on earth would I do?

One morning an ad appeared in *The New York Times,* and it said, "Young men wanted. Young men capable of close observation. No particular scholastic requirements. Men of all-round ability," etc. And I thought, "Well now, that's me."

"Please write a letter," said the ad. So I wrote a letter stating my experience and ability, and nothing happened for about ten days. In the meanwhile, I had virtually got a job as an investigator for a surety company, investigating criminal defaults around in brokerage houses. I hadn't actually started to work. Meanwhile, at my grandfather's insistence, I had decided to abandon engineering, which I had never finished anyway, and made up my mind to study law. And by this time I was going to law school at St. Lawrence University, then known as the Brooklyn Law School, every night. So this investigation job promised well. It would take me away from a desk and make my time more flexible and my own, and it had a lot of appeal. And all this had built up as a very happy prospect, when I suddenly got a letter from the Edison Laboratories, from Mr. Edison himself, hoping that I would come to East Orange and undergo an examination, a qualifying exam for some sort of employment. Maybe it was blinder than that. I forgot. Maybe we got there before we realized what it was, but would we come to East Orange, anyway.

So I went over there, found myself at the Edison Laboratories, a couple of score of people were there. The employment manager had picked out about a dozen of us, and he sent us to another building and up a flight of stairs and into a long, oblong room with very rough furniture, some very plain, cheap tables; over in one corner a cheap and battered desk, at which was sitting none other than Thomas

Alva Edison. And along the walls there was some laboratory equipment and drains and sinks and one thing and another, and this was obviously the old man's place of business.

So he sat us down at the tables and handed us out a questionnaire. I remember the one we got had 286 questions. And in one question they would want to know what was the diameter of the moon, and the next question would be what are overtones on a stringed instrument, and the next question was, where do they make the most shoes, and the next question would be, what kind of wood do they use for oil-barrel staves, and it just covered the gamut. And the obvious idea was to see whether you'd been observant in your reading and in your observation of things in life in general.

. . . over in one corner a cheap and battered desk, at which was sitting none other than Thomas Alva Edison.

Well, the afternoon wore on, and people finished their papers and turned them in, and I hadn't finished. I answered all the questions I could immediately and then went over, because a lot of them were capable of estimates—comparative populations and some scientific things could be estimated and others you could remember if you kept working at it. So I answered a very large proportion of the questions in some fashion or other, and the old man came over and asked if I found the exam hard, and I said, yes, that I thought it was very difficult.

In the meanwhile, I'd had quite a glimpse of him. He'd

been one of my heroes as an aspiring electrical engineer. I remember how a former pupil of his, one of the Japanese nobility, had come in to pay him a visit, and then an assistant came in with a bar of platinum, which would be ruinously expensive if they were to plane it and so spoil it. And the old man burst into a volley of oaths that, "By Christ, this thing is going to be planed and you do it, you do as I tell you, see," showing that he was an old martinet on that side of it.

Well, at any rate, I came back, and hearing nothing from the Edison Laboratories, I went to work for this surety company, the U.S. Fidelity and Guaranty Company, on William Street in New York, as a criminal investigator of defaults, mostly in stock exchange firms in Wall Street, and continued the study of law at night.

Meanwhile, Lois and I had moved to 142 Amity Street, not in the least a fashionable neighborhood anymore, it being largely occupied by Syrians. And our landlords were man and wife, he a fellow who had come here from Syria to make his fortune and indeed he had, starting first as a tin peddler and then putting his money in real estate, which is now the Coney Island Boardwalk. And he had a large, assorted hardware store on Vesey Street. And they let us the top floor of an old brownstone, to which we had to walk up several flights and live under that tin roof.

Well, Lois has a vast ability to make places habitable and beautiful, and here we were. She was working, she was getting about $150 a month, and I was getting about the same, and the rent was depressed, and we began to save money. And then, as I traveled around Wall Street, I began to get acquainted with stockbrokers and began to read on economics and began to be interested in the market and sensed that there might be a shortcut.

Meanwhile, however, there had been a temptation to turn in the other direction, because one night quite late, the bell rang downstairs and up came a reporter from *The New York Times*, who announced to me that I had been one of the winners of the Edison test, and he wanted to know all about me and, of course, I felt very pleasantly elated by all this, and after a while I got a letter from the old boy, wishing me to come in as a researcher in their acoustics department. I'd shown a good deal of knowledge of sound and acoustics in stringed instruments and that sort of thing . . . was beginning to give him a hell of a rub. But I never went and continued on the course that I just outlined to you.

And life was very happy, but the drinking built up all the time. . . . And then, of course, we were in the Prohibition era, and there were batches of beer and I got the habit of going in the fall to buy grapes and pressing them out in big crocks, which I would drink before they were half fermented. There was a great deal of that. In fact, when I—on a final exam at law school, where I went three years nights—I failed it because I was too drunk and had to come back in the fall and make up, and I did make it up in the fall and then demanded my diploma, which they would never give me because I was supposed to appear at the following commencement for it, but I never appeared and my diploma as a graduate lawyer still rests in the Brooklyn Law School. I never went back for it. I must do that before I die.

At any rate, in this period I began, as I say, to get in circulation amongst the stockbrokers and wonder why so many people lost so much money and wondered why they acted on so little investigation. And suddenly it dawned on me that I ought to make a very good investigator of security values. By this time I'd had a lot of experience with the seamy side of New York; I'd been through a criminal investigation experience that tied me up with Burns Detective Agency; I was a half-baked engineer; I was interested in scientific things; I had a flare with people; I had the shrewd Yankee idea, so I thought, that you'd better look in the horse's mouth before you buy him. So I

> . . . my diploma as a graduate lawyer still rests in the Brooklyn Law School.

began to canvass my stockbroker friends on this matter of being hired as an investigator, . . . and they all laughed at me, and I persisted with the idea; all of a sudden financial tycoons became my heroes, and I began to read up on all that sort of business. I began to get up on accounting and read lots of books on economics. I continued my interest in radio, and I built one of the very early superheterodyne sets that were around among amateurs there on Amity Street. Then I began to build sets for sale. We made a little something that way. There was an attic under this roof we could use.

But I got more and more obsessed that the stock market was the place, and the thing to do was go out and really investigate these companies.

Well, as I say, we couldn't get up any interest, despite the fact that I proved that Lois and I had already been making money. As a matter of fact, we have been saving by depressing our living about 125 bucks a month, and we had put this into one and two and three shares of this, that, and the other, and that process was begun way back in 1921, which was then one of the bottoms of the market, and we put it into mostly electrical stuff, utilities and this, that, and the other thing. They all showed very big markup by 1924, when I got this hex that investigation of securities was the thing.

At that time Lois and I owned, I think, two shares of General Electric, which people thought we had paid a fabulous sum for, being as they cost us $180 a share. Those same shares on split-ups became worth four or five thousand dollars a share. But never mind, I thought that was pretty good. So I proposed to Lois that we go out and investigate the General Electric Company and bring the results back to Wall Street. Rather audacious, wasn't it?

So, believe it or not, Lois and I persuaded ourselves that we ought to give up our jobs and go out to investigate such securities as we had and make reports on those, and send them back to Wall Street, where I had begun to have some friends. Among these friends was one Frank Shaw, . . . and he started off in Wall Street, a shrewd Maine Yankee with a little bit of his wife's capital, at J. K. Rice, first as an over-the-counter trader and then as an operator in his own right, and was already worth a million dollars and mighty well knew what I was talking about.

However, I had no assurance from him when we started off. We just naturally started. Well, how did we start? As I say, we didn't have a great deal of money, and that was tied up in securities, so we took a motorcycle and sidecar, which we had bought to run out to the beach on weekends; we took my army locker and strapped it on the back and put in some suits and clothes; we bought an explorer's tent, very waterproof with a cloth bottom, about seven by seven. I took along a full set of *Moody's Manuals,* and blankets, and a gasoline cookstove. And we both gave up our jobs, gave up the apartment, stored our things, and headed for Schenectady to investigate the General Electric Company. That's how my Wall Street career started.

Well, of course everybody thought that we were utterly out of our minds, but there were other motivations. Meanwhile the drinking had got worse and worse, and although I couldn't be impressed with its seriousness, except now and then when there was a humiliating episode, Lois was greatly bothered and worried, and she thought something like this might get me out of it.

So off we went, and I think we started off with one hundred dollars in cash, and we made a resolve that we, one or both of us, would work every time that cash ran out and [get] another grubstake to travel to another place to look into another company, meanwhile living in the tent. By this time Lois was a hardened camper and so was I already; it wasn't so audacious from that point of view. We well knew what to do and how to handle that.

So we go to Schenectady, having first spent a little time over in Dorset, where my grandfather had just died, my Grandfather Griffith. Parenthetically, I never mentioned Grandmother Griffith in the account so far. She came from a family of twelve children, and they were pioneer stock only to the account that her ancestor, a Bock, came from

France as a stowaway in time to fight the battle of Stony Point. There was a neurotic streak in that family too, but Grandmother was a very stable, temperate sort of person, although she had a sister who was a depressive. She was very sweet and good to me, but somehow she never evoked the love and adulation that I gave my grandfather.

At any rate, we left East Dorset to brace the General Electric Company in Schenectady. We arrived at the General Electric Company. I put on my only good suit of clothes, walking into the main offices and announced that I was a stockholder, and that I wanted to know this, that, and the other thing.

Well, I got very courteously received. Meanwhile, too, I had put on my overalls and tried to get a job in the place, to see the inside. And they allowed me a tourist inspection of it. . . . Well, they didn't really know what to make of me, and I could see that. I told this naive story of being a small shareholder, and they didn't know whether to talk little or talk much. And right then it began to be evident that I had a flare for extracting information. Because I did get a couple of pieces of information that were worth a little. But I couldn't get work there.

. . . I had a flare for extracting information.

Well, we tried the Adirondack Light and Power. We tried everything that would have any bearing on what I was trying to do. Meanwhile we were living on the farm of some Poles, nearly all of the family working in the General Electric plant—the old man and the old woman carrying on the place. And we were running out of our one hundred dollars.

So we just had to have some more money, and it was haying time and we saw an ad in a local paper, put there by a farmer in Scotia, which I think is just out of Schenectady to the west, and he wanted help during harvest.

So it was pouring rain when we saw that ad, and we packed up in the rain so as to be sure to beat all other applicants to the job, and through a blinding thunderstorm we drove across Schenectady and out to Scotia, and arrived there (we had overall suits that were waterproof). We arrived there pretty bedraggled, and looked up this farmer who, we saw, wasn't very successful. His wife was [of] good, old pioneering stock, but he had only been a coachman . . . and a turnkey in the Schenectady jail and wasn't doing too well with the farm. They were both damn hard workers but awful dumb about farming.

Well, they looked us over and were very reluctant to hire us. They were very reluctant to hire us, but I insisted that I could milk and came from East Dorset, Vermont, and knew farming, and Lois claimed that she could cook, which was a damned lie. She had a cookbook, but she thought she could cook for a farm, and so we began getting up at four in the morning and Lois, out of the cookbook, began doing the cooking and that left the old woman and the old man Goldfoot, for such was his name, and me out into the field.

Well, I had a little mechanical flare, and the teeth were out of his horse rake, and the hay fork in the barn wasn't working, and I fixed up this and that and the other thing, and Lois cooked to suit them all. And we stayed there exactly a month, for which we got our board and seventy-five dollars.

The first ten days about killed me, but then I began to get in condition and even had wind after milking at night and supper to sit up for three or four hours reading the *Moody's Manuals,* looking for financial opportunities. However, one turned up right there. We discovered that this farm was adjacent to some farms owned by the General Electric Company, on which stood their research laboratories in radio. So I got in the habit of running over and getting acquainted with the boys evenings, you know, around the lab, and pretty soon I was around inside the place and boy, with what I knew about radio I could see plenty. I got a preview of the whole radio industry five and ten years away.

I saw the beginning of sound motion pictures. I saw superheterodyne radios and console sets and magnets and tone reproduction and two-way telephonic communication . . . and all kinds of things. With a little imagination you just got a preview of what that aspect of General Electric is today. Of course, you could only write about it in general terms, so I commenced to ship some reports to Wall Street about what was going on up there. It was just a break, and I fell right into it.

Well, I had made a pretty deep impression upon the husband of Lois's friend, Frank Shaw, and upon his firm. Meanwhile I'd seen that the farmers were using a pile of cement, that a building boom was starting up (this was about '24); I could also see an immense amount of cement going into concrete roads, which were heavy duty and were replacing everything else, so I figured there was an uptrend in cement. So I went through every cement company in *Moody's Manuals* and lit on a little one called Giant Portland Cement, whose stock was listed on the Philadelphia Exchange, and whose capitalization—market value plus underlying debt—per barrel of production was the lowest, and apparently it had been through a hard time and had been a mess, and I said, "Maybe that's it." And when we got seventy-five dollars and finished our month with Goldfoot, and sent in the report on General Electric, we pulled up stakes for Egypt, Pennsylvania.

I put on my old clothes, I went down [and got] an estimate on what it was costing them in the quarry operation.

I got inside the plant and found out how much coal they were burning to make a barrel of cement. I read the meters on their power input and saw what that was doing. I saw how much stuff they were shipping. I took their financial statements, and with this information and the discovery that they [had] just installed a hell of a lot more efficient equipment—supersynchronic motors and all that stuff—that just meant worlds to production costs. I got it figured out that they were making cement for less than a dollar a barrel, which was way down the line in costs, and still the stock was dawdling around in the Philadelphia market for very low figures, down around fifteen dollars a share.

So I send a wire in to the broker, and I buy myself five shares of Giant Portland Cement, and I put on the good clothes, and I walk into the front office. Well, this time it's a little company, you know, and the guy can't make me out, and I'm a stockholder, . . . and I get talking to him, and all of a sudden I confront him with my estimate, and how I got it.

So I walked out around there, and I said, "Isn't this about so?" And then he said what I hoped. He pulled his complete cost sheets out of his drawer and I saw them, and he said he just sold his stock, it was too high. He was earning money at the rate of five dollars a share and the stock was selling for fifteen dollars. He had seen it come up from about three so he thought it was too high. Holy smoke! . . . I had him cold. There wasn't any question about it. I could prove it.

So [I] hotfooted it back to New York, went to this firm, and I said, "Now here is the situation, and I want an interest

in it. . . ." I afterward learned they bought five thousand
shares of stock, and they carried me for one hundred shares
at twenty. Now, this was my first experience with a one-
hundred-share lot.

Meanwhile, all this buying had pulled the stock up to
about twenty-five, so I said to them, "Well, now, I've got a
five-hundred-dollar profit. . . . Have you got some things
you would like to have me look into?"

Well, yes, there would be the Aluminum Company of
America, the American Cyanamid Company, the . . . U.S.
Cast Iron Pipe, the Florida real estate situation, etc., etc.

So Lois and I set sail for [the] South, with winter coming
on. And we go all down through there, looking at one situation and another, meanwhile drawing money against the
advancing price of Giant Portland Cement, which finally
wound up at seventy-five bucks a share.

Well, come spring we turned north again, meanwhile
turning in all these reports. By this time my friend had
moved into a brokerage shop and become a pretty big operator and got in a lot of money, and he had a lot of speculative trusts. I afterward learned they had about $10 million
available, and so they gave me a grubstake. They gave me a
credit of 20 thousand bucks . . . and I began to go to
Canada to look over the new aluminum development up
there. And I was down and made an examination in
Muscle Shoals [Alabama]. I was all over the place and into
all kinds of industries and kept turning in these reports and

had a credit with which to buy stocks for $20 thousand.

Boy, we were right in on the ground floor and holy smoke! When 1928 blew around I was a tycoon, see, and they thought I was just wonderful. Meanwhile, the drinking—up and up and up. And the crowd down there, hell, we'd—the minute the three o'clock bell sounded—we'd be out to the speakeasy. I'd be pretty much out of commission at Fourteenth Street and completely lose my wits at Fifty-ninth . . . drop $500 out of the window and crawl under a subway gate to [get] back to Brooklyn.

Meanwhile, Lois and I had moved into one apartment, but that wasn't big enough. We knocked out the wall between that and another apartment and things were expanding. Meanwhile the drinking was going up and up and up, but I was making so god-damn much money and that was a symbol of importance, and I was Mr. Big, and I was in with the big-time speculator clique as their number-one investigator, so what the hell! Do you see?

. . . holy smoke! When 1928 blew around I was a tycoon . . .

Meanwhile, I'm beginning to get terrible hangovers, and that was a pretty godawful episode. In those days, of course, I was drinking for paranoid reasons. I was drinking to dream greater dreams of power, dreams of domination. Money to me was never a symbol of security, it was a symbol of prestige and power, and I began to look forward to the time when I would sit on this board of directors, or that board of directors, and the other board of directors. J. P. Morgan and the First National Bank were, you know, my heroes.

You asked if the drinking incapacitated me. Yes. Well, it began to worry my partners very greatly. On the other hand, I was practically never out on the job. I could stand any amount of this night business and still get around in the morning and get drunk properly at three the next afternoon. Sometimes out on a trip I embarrassed them by getting crosswise of management, by getting too drunk, and by the time '28 and '29 rolled around and I'd got to be Mr. Big myself, and they wanted me to pool my money—which had pyramided out of the $20 thousand—with theirs. I wasn't going to get tied up with them.

So, by this time I had got the golf mania and went to Vermont to learn to play golf. Semiretirement during '29. Fiddling while Rome burned. Of course, it was in this period, beginning about 1927, that Lois got frightfully worried, and we would take trips, and she would arrange weekends. Besides, I behaved so badly on parties that her friends would have, that—even though some of them drank a good deal—they couldn't stand for me. And, of course, I was very loudmouthed when I drank, and I felt a terrible inferiority to some of her people, and the boy from the country had come in and made more money than they'd ever seen, and that was the theme of my talk, and people increasingly just couldn't take it. We were in the process already of being isolated, that process being mitigated only by the fact that we were making money and more money, do you see?

And then we went to Vermont in 1929, when I broke up with my friend Shaw and his friend, and I determined after a summer of golf I was going to be a lone wolf, maybe the Wolf of Wall Street. . . . And in that time, you see, it was supreme egotism and omnipotence and utter confidence, and I knew I was going to be a number-one man in Wall Street. Only it didn't turn out that way.

While I was in Vermont in the summer of '29, the market got pretty shaky, and I came back here [to New York City] very briefly to attend to business. And by that time I had some pet operations of my own. One of them was in the stock of a small company called Penick and Ford. It had been a molasses business belonging to a New Orleans family . . . and that had been combined with a kind of a broken-down corn products plant. But young Bedford, the son of old man Bedford, who had founded the corn products company, had moved into the picture, and a lot of stock from the [molasses business] was floating around the market. And the Bedfords, as they always did, were telling about how high the price was, and I made one of these inside job investigations on that deal and figured out that with that kind of management, that thing was really going places.

Meanwhile, I got terribly frightened about the high prices of some of these automobile and radio and utility stocks and, although the future of aluminum seemed to be then so terrific, and of nickel, that I could still hang on there, but I was still looking for something more conservative. So I

> Characteristically, I did the job just in reverse of everybody else.

kind of focused on this thing, and became in a very small way on my own hook, a sort of a market operator.

Characteristically, I did the job just in reverse of everybody else. I went on the theory that I would go out and sell my friends this stock. In other words, encourage them to buy it on the open market. I got a hold of this specialist in the stock. I sold him a bill of goods, that is after accumulating my own line. And then I figured that if I did enough advertising with this around, and solid selling, that every time we got a bad market setback, I could bring in enough buying to peg the damn thing. It wasn't too big, only four hundred thousand shares, which by this time had only gotten into the forties. (I'd started in with it at about twenty the year before.) That I could peg it and so protect myself and that would enable me to run on a pretty small shoestring. In other words, I could carry lines of thousands of shares of it myself.

And, sure enough, in the spring of 1929, there was a hell of a crack in the market and, boy, [I] let that thing down five points, and I got thousands of shares of it into my friends' hands and meanwhile pegged the price and protected myself. So I thought, "Well, you put your friends in on the dip instead of selling it to them on the bulges and that gives them a wonderful break, and meanwhile they're protected. I'm not trying to trade on them and make money that way. And we've got a long, full operation good enough for quite a while yet." And that was the state of affairs back in '29.

Well, up in the country I began to get wobbly in August. I was drunk most of the while and playing golf and fooling around and making an impression on the local bank with the size of my checks in and out of there, and besides, I was associating with the elite of Manchester, them city folks that used to despise my kind, you know, and getting a big kick out of it.

Meanwhile, Lois's apprehension is going up and up and up, and again I was either booze or golf and, you know, she's kind of an also-ran. Poor girl, it's been her lot ever since. However, we had many happy times together. It wasn't all bad at all. Of course, as a golfer, I would soon catch up with [Walter] Hagen. And that was a morning, noon, and night business. Two rounds a day, plus practice as soon as it was daylight, and then until dark was approaching, and I never could learn to play golf. My crooked arm spoiled it, and I suspect the booze had put my coordination on the bum.

Anyway, in August the market got—I don't know, I didn't like it. And I went down and I wanted to unload some of my stuff. Well, gee, the market was so cleaned up and so scarce of this stock that if I were to unload any, it would knock hell out of it, and yet I felt I ought to. The result was that I had one very well-heeled friend, and he said, "Well, hell, set up an account for no money in it, and I'll guarantee it and you can unload a jag of that stuff into that account, and I'll guarantee it. If it goes down, we'll keep it for you. This'll work out." And he wanted me to do that so that it wouldn't disturb the market and hurt other friends of mine, so I did it and meanwhile lightened my own account.

Well, holy smoke, then came the crash. And the first day of the crash I started for Montreal, where we had a hell of a buy—I had a big buying power, and I got quite a lot of buying put into stock that day. The thing had been up to fifty-five, and I think that night it hit a bottom of forty-two, and that was getting real bad for me, and recovered somewhat on buying I got into it.

The next night, of course, I'm drunk as hell, and I fish out of the ticker tape basket in the Hotel Windsor a piece of tape which says, "Penick and Ford—32." That was me. I'm kaput—everything and all the rest, I didn't have much of anything else. I mean, I'd just been making a big play in that. That was my lone wolf operation.

Well, here we were, hung high and dry in Montreal. So I came back to New York and the apartment we lived in—the double apartment that had the wall knocked out, so as to make a grandiose, double-sized living room and a double dose of bedrooms, bathrooms, kitchens, everything. That apartment on Livingston Street was hung up on a long-term lease, and I had gone to them a year or two before and said, "I'm in a very hazardous business. I've got plenty of money now, I want to pay all this lease in advance," which was chicken feed. And they wouldn't take it, and now came the crash, and I'm just . . . broke.

. . . I'm at loggerheads with a lot of people, and I told a lot of people off and all that sort of business.

Meanwhile, I'm drinking like a fish, and the minute my money went, the confidence in me was suddenly zero. Meanwhile, I'm at loggerheads with a lot of people, and I told a lot of people off and all that sort of business. So, boy, were we really up against it. Well, a friend of mine in Montreal said, "Come on up and I'll give you a chance."

Greenshields and Company up there, good old Dick Johnson. So, Lois and I start for Montreal. We land in a little dingy apartment out on Girouard Street about Christmastime. This friend gives me a little bit of a drawing account, just enough to carry that by, and we start in Montreal.

Well, gee, I'm there only a little while when I [run] across a remittance man from England who really has some dough, and I sell him on Penick and Ford, and he gives me a credit of five thousand bucks. Well, I had a lot of friends, including the specialist, whose fifty thousand shares had been taken over by Case-Pomeroy at twenty-two, and I started right back into it right there, see. And in the recovery which took place in the spring of '30, the damned stock got back clear to fifty-five, so I pyramided this all the way up again, see. And in nothing flat I'm living in the Glen Eagles Apartment . . . overlooking the St. Lawrence and about fifty miles of Vermont besides, and the goose is hanging high again, and I'm drunker and drunker and drunker, and finally that really blows up with a hell of a bang. And boy, our furniture is moved into storage, I'm hung up with this apartment, with the other one in Brooklyn, I'm drunk, my friend has to let me out, I had to borrow the money to get out of town, leaving our furniture there. Well, that about gets us up to the crash period. You had enough?

Bill W.

Ed and I just had a good laugh about the Wall Street days of the last record, in a general way, over my obliquity to what was really going on, but as we just replayed the record, it is all too clear that I reverted to type. The whole tone of the thing sounds like I was in a barroom pounding on the bar, talking big deals, financial omnipotence and power, and it has a shoddy undertone and the old power drive is there in all its. . . . [I] would certainly have a field day with these recordings as they've gone thus far. We had just reached the point in the narrative where I'd gone over the edge and was hitting the downslope that by 1934 was to lead me into the Valley of the Shadow.

By this time, the fall of 1930, I caught occasional glimpses of the downslope leading to the Valley of the Shadow. But I could still turn and look the other way, even though I had been deeply shocked by the calamity of the 1929 crash and now the dismissal of my good friend Dick Johnson.

Poor Lois, meanwhile, had gone home to Brooklyn to join her mother whilst I cleaned up odds and ends in Montreal in order to make good our escape from the scene of this last failure. Even at the very end with much to do, I still couldn't keep sober. I remember getting very drunk, falling into an argument with the hotel detective. Being thrown into jail, the judge letting me off easy the next morning. By noon I was sodden again and had struck up a comradeship with another alcoholic, a very unusual type, a tinhorn confidence-man variety.

Somehow, I'll never know, we got across the border into Vermont and thence down to a beautiful camp that belonged to Lois's parents at North Dorset, on dear old Emerald Lake. I woke up there in the company of this stranger, with an atrocious hangover, and it took about every cent I had left to export him once more northward to Montreal. All the while it was turning cold, now being the fall of 1930. Lois came up to join me at the camp, to ponder over whatever the next course of action might be.

By this time I really began to appreciate her intense devotion, courage, and still-high confidence in me. After a season of no alcohol, we advanced again upon New York to recoup our fortunes.

During the late '20s, after painful episodes, I would often try to stop drinking. Lois deeply sensed that something was grievously wrong with me, and at times I think I did. But in that term I believe I would have periods of dryness more to please her and always in anticipation of starting again in more moderation and with control. But following the Montreal debacle I think I tried hard for the first time to stop because I really wanted to stop.

On our return to Brooklyn, Lois's parents took us in. They were truly a marvelous couple. Her mother was one of the greatest souls I have ever known. Her capacity for the kind of love that demands no reward for nearly everything and everybody was quite past belief and understanding. She came of a fine old Brooklyn family and had married a rising doctor, Dr. Clark Burnham. He had come to Brooklyn in his youth from Pennsylvania.

Even in his advancing years he was an exceedingly handsome individual, dressed immaculately and was as courtly in his speech and manner as anyone I ever knew. But underneath his politeness there was an extreme aggressiveness and a terrific domination that affected the whole family life. This without his in the least intending it or anyone realizing what was going on. Even in late life he was a man of immense energy. Nearing eighty, I saw him one day at Boro Hall, running up three flights of elevated stairs, two steps at a time, entirely effortless. He was a diet expert and brought himself [from] a state of invalidism as a young man when he had rheumatic fever into his present estate by eating about a third of what everybody else did and chewing that, Fletcher-style, hours at a time. A rare character he was and extremely kind to me at all times.

By now Lois's sisters and brothers had departed the house at 182 Clinton Street. These were, by the way, Rogers, next oldest to her, Lois being the elder of the family, and there was Barbara, Catherine, and Lyman.

For a time I deeply felt [the] humiliation of my failures and really resolved not to drink again. It was mighty hard for me too, erstwhile the great provider, to accept the hospitality of the in-laws.

I secured a job as an investigator for the Stanley Statistics of New York, and presently the old power drive was on.

At first I made a little headway with this organization. Then came the first drink and it crept up on me. However, I attended to my work pretty well for perhaps a year. But I was impatient and very restless, for the salary was only a hundred dollars a week. It seemed like a small sum to me then. I was heavily in debt. The crash had left me $60 thousand in arrears. A few of the creditors were pushing me. Nevertheless, I still had unbounded confidence in my future, and I can well remember the disdain with which I regarded those suicides who had leaped from the towers of high finance after the crash.

It was mighty hard for me too, erstwhile the great provider, to accept the hospitality of the in-laws.

But the drinking kept up, and finally a barroom brawl in which some thugs got hold of some of my papers, from which they learned my business address and used them as a basis of threatening me over the phone, was something which looked like it might turn into blackmail. Whether this was the immediate cause of my discharge from Stanley Statistics, I don't know. But one day I was abruptly fired.

This was another very severe blow and although Lois and her family stood by with their usual love, confidence, and fortitude, I was really badly shaken. I began to canvass my few friends in the Street who had survived the crash, but I found their confidence in me had really oozed out years before. Now that I was penniless and obviously in deep trouble with liquor, they had nothing for me and surely they could not be blamed for that.

To bring in something, Lois began to work in a department store, at Macy's, to be exact. She got a job in the furniture department, as the result of a course in interior decoration she'd taken years before. By this time she began to be very deeply affected by my drinking, but this only increased her devotion and love. With few exceptions, she was always at great pains to hide her inner fears, which were becoming very great and disturbing.

The time had come when I had become really unemployable. I sat about brokerage shops during the day in order to present the appearance of being at work. I was nothing but a typical hanger-on waiting for the main chance, [like Dickens's Mr. Micawber]. Now and then I would get a market idea for a quick turn, sell it to some small-time operator with a little capital, and bring home a few hundred dollars. Or at least the remainder of a few hundred dollars. Most of the money by now would go to pay up the speakeasy bills in order to be sure of a line of fresh credit when I should next run out of money. Night after night I was appearing at Clinton Street very drunk. I had become, too, a lone drinker, partly because I preferred it and partly because none of my Wall Street companions, however hard that is, cared anymore for my company.

Whenever possible I bought a fifth of gin in the morning and nibbled at it discreetly during business hours while I watched the market and hung around one brokerage shop or another. I knew I had to keep sober enough in these places not to get thrown out. The gin would stimulate my imagination so I spent most of my time persuading people to enter this little deal or that with the indifferent result I've just noted. At market closing time I would cadge a few drinks from my better-heeled acquaintances, on those occasions when they would have anything to do with me. I'd borrow a few dollars if I could and on leaving them would repair to the nearest bootlegger, get a bottle, and sometimes would ride up and down the subway for hours, nipping away, appearing at Clinton Street at any old time.

This sort of thing went on all through 1931 and into the summer of 1932. When a little money came in I would go on sprees, being out of commission for several days at a time. I began to understand what real hangovers were like and sometimes bordered on delirium. Upstairs I would lie in bed and drink while Lois was at work. How her dear parents put up with me is more than I can conceive.

At this stage I began to show definite impairment. Usually I had been a fairly amiable and docile drunk given to excessive babbling before blackouts. But now when anybody expostulated, I began to turn violent and talked such gibberish that people about me were frightened to death. The demon was now moving into full possession. Nevertheless I was still to have one more financial opportunity.

My brother-in-law, Gardner Swentzel, Catherine Burnham's husband, was also in the Street, and notwithstanding the crash and the unending decline in the market, he still retained

. . . I made a superhuman effort to restrain myself during business hours and watched my opportunity.

many friends and was able to get along as a customer's man in a firm that had Morgan connections. In early '32, I began to frequent his shop. . . . Mr. J. B. Taylor, also Mr. Bates, I think, were close friends among the Morgan partners. Indeed, I believe Mr. Taylor was an old friend of J. P. himself. These folks were, of course, very close to the American Can Company. It was sort of . . . in the Morgan orbit.

Of course this shop [catered to] conservative and wealthy clientele. Realizing the latent possibilities, I made a superhuman effort to restrain myself during business hours and watched my opportunity.

Through my brother-in-law I struck up an acquaintance with a friend of his, who was no other than Arthur Wheeler, the only son of the president of the American Can Company. Art was somewhat of a drinker himself, but by no means an alcoholic. He didn't care a fig about anybody's habits so long as they had brains and could tend to business. So he sized me up cautiously for a while and finally made up his mind that I had ideas that he would use. For my own part, I could see that he had capital and in back of him there was any amount of it. Our acquaintance ripened little by little and I was soon included in with a retired banker of Chicago, Frank Winans, who operated for his own account at Taylor Bates. Frank also had wide connections and became attracted to some of the ideas I managed to present.

Actually, with the stock market approaching its all-time low, good and persuasive ideas or long-pull speculations were not hard to come by. If one could overcome his fears, have capital and patience, there could be a fortune in the recovery that was bound to come one day. America was rapidly approaching the state where a turn simply had to be made. Either there would be a wholesale inflation of the currency, which would result in rising prices, or there would be a recovery such as came out of the panic of [18]97 or [18]93. . . .

Meanwhile, the market value of many securities had fallen way below the net worth of the enterprises, sometimes as far as one-half or one-third. From my extensive firsthand knowledge of a great many concerns, . . . I persuaded Arthur Wheeler and Frank Winans, with some wealthy friends, to enter a long-term speculative syndicate. While they were certainly going to operate on the side with their own cash, they put enough chips into the deal to ensure me a great comeback with the third interest I was given in it.

I was utterly overjoyed. On the comeback, over the years I could really become rich in company like this. One simply couldn't fail. My friends, though tolerant, were nevertheless shrewd. Their investigation of me showed plenty of liquor trouble, and they were frank enough to come to me and say that they were scared to death of this aspect of things.[4]

---

4. Editor's note—At this point in Bill's dialogue, he pauses to change the tape, and adds: "This is side 2 of record number 4, reminiscences talked out with Ed Bierstadt, Hotel Bedford, September 2, 1954. Beg pardon, Ed says it's the third of September. I'm so excited about the prospects of getting back to writing, I forget about the passage of

Of course, I had anticipated this. In fact, I had looked at my drinking as squarely as I possibly could. I guess this was the first time that I realized I was out of control and deeply wanted, for my own sake and for the sake of everybody, to stop forever. My new friends exhorted me, saying that with an opportunity such as the one I now had, how could I think of letting it slip by way of the bottle. Eagerly, and with the deepest of sincerity, I agreed with them and I stopped. I stopped cold and really thought I was done with it. My friends were cautious and they were conservative, so they took out some insurance against possible relapse in signing up the syndicate agreement with me. I entered into a contract, . . . which could be by its nature indefinite, [and] I pledged myself not to drink. And the penalty, even if I took a single drink of alcohol, would be the loss of all my interest in this new enterprise of such immense promise. I signed the agreement and drew a tremendous sigh of relief. I was utterly confident and plunged forward into the work.

Lois and I and the whole family had a time of great happiness. At last the corner had been turned, the long night was ended, the sun was just coming over the horizon, and the zenith was the limit.

the days. On side 1 I have just been telling about the marvelous opportunity to recoup my financial fortunes which came to me at the lowest spot of America's economic history, in May and June of 1932."

So things went on for the next two or three months. Utterly absorbed now, I found I had very little urge to drink. I was amazed at the lack of temptation. Word soon got around Wall Street that I had stopped. One day an old acquaintance, who had refused to have anything to do with me, called me up and asked me if it were really true that I had stopped for good. I assured him that this was so. "Well," said he, "maybe for old time's sake you'd like to do a little job for me. I know you are your own boss and your time is your own, and I don't think your partners would mind. So won't you go over to the Pathé Laboratory at Bound Brook, New Jersey, in company with some engineers, and look over a new photographic process down there?"[5]

. . . I found I had very little urge to drink. I was amazed at the lack of temptation.

I arrived at Bound Brook in the company of several engineers. We sent down to the Pathé place, and I was so happy about it all, especially over the fact that even a brief period of sobriety had attracted my friends to me again.

---

5. Editor's note—At this point, the dialogue ends and Bill starts again, with the following: "This is Sunday, September 4, 1954. Ed and I are now in the studio at Bedford Hills, and I think we'll try to finish up this side of record [4]. Here goes the narrative."

After supper, the boys broke out a deck of cards and commenced to play poker. I was invited in, but couldn't join
because I'd never had any interest in cards, not the slightest.
This was not a little curious, for my Wall Street operations
were partly in the nature of gambling. So I just sat and
looked on. But this wasn't the only thing they produced. A
jug of applejack mysteriously appeared from somewhere. It
was called "Jersey lightning." They poured me a drink and
handed it over. I most easily refused. In the mind's eye, as
soon as the applejack showed up, I could see Lois working in
that department, I could see the contract I had signed, and
one of my special prides was honor of signature, and I could
see the future, glowing and rosy, stretching out straight
ahead. I simply couldn't miss. So, I turned the applejack
down with great ease. It was really a cinch, I thought.

The evening wore on. Now and again they would renew
their offer of a drink. Each time, very easily, I turned the
liquor aside. Indeed, I once explained to them that I was a
person who couldn't take it, an alcoholic.

As the clock neared twelve, I found myself getting awfully
bored just looking on and I remember slipping into a sort of
a daydream state. My mind traversed back to the glad, bad
days of World War I. My first experience with French claret,
the Bordeaux white wine, then remembrances about service
over there, then cognac and a whole list of other liquors that
I once enjoyed began to troop through my mind, clearly
labeled. This pleasing reverie continued for a spell, and in

some mysterious way it deepened. If only one could turn the clock back, I thought. There were certainly wonderful days ahead, but none had been more full of joy than some I had spent in the army. High adventure, the electric thrill of champagne, good talk in the cafés. Well, I had seen life, hadn't I?

Then a notion struck me. I had been passed applejack, better known as Jersey lightning. As everybody knows, it's a distilled cider with a terrific wallop. Suddenly I remembered with not a little consternation that never in my drinking career, which had included nearly every sort of known booze, including bay rum and smoke, I had never tasted Jersey lightning. Judging by the fun the boys were having, that appeared to be a serious omission. I'd missed a real experience no doubt. And so the rationalization about this Jersey lightning went on abuilding until presently someone made another attempt, handed me a glass, and my only thought was this, "Well, I guess one bolt of Jersey lightning couldn't hurt me much," and I bolted it down.

The moment the fiery liquor hit bottom, I panicked just briefly. I thought, "Great guns, I've broken my contract. This can't go on." Then came the next rationalization. "Well, old boy, you've had one drink. The contract can't be broken any more by two, or maybe a third, and then you'll go to bed." Meanwhile, Barleycorn grabbed hold. Dry for three months, my imagination soared.

I can recollect no more of that evening. Of course, I must have taken plenty of drinks after that. The next morning I arose with a terrible hangover. To be more accurate, I don't think I arose at all. Instead I sent for the bellboy. He brought me another crock of lightning. I took some, cautiously now mixing it with water, before I realized that I had to go to work. Just a few eye openers, just enough to get going, that was the idea.

The next thing I remembered it was evening. I dimly sensed interludes in which I pulled at the jug. I was lying on the bed, drinking all day. I summoned the bellboy again.

This went on, I think, for three days, and then, as from a great distance, I heard a bell ring and finally woke to the fact that it was the telephone at my bedside. I raised the receiver. At the other end was my friend Art, the key man in my new financial empire to be. He was saying, "Bill, we've heard all about it. I'm terribly sorry, but the deal is off." I knew he meant it. Even my numb senses reeled under the impact of that one. As I lie here dictating I can still feel it. And, for the first time, when in one of these debacles, I found myself desperately frightened. Why? Oh, why had I done this? Why at eight o'clock was I perfectly sane? Why at eight o'clock could I see Lois, my contract, and the bright road ahead? Only to have that all pushed into the background by the crazy rationalization that I'd never had a drink of applejack.

This was more than habit, this was more than compulsion. This was actually insanity in a certain sense.

This was more than habit, this was more than compulsion.

This was actually insanity in a certain sense. Somehow I got home, still pretty tight. Because she hadn't heard from me, Lois was getting terribly worried, and now she knew the worst. I hadn't felt so ashamed, so utterly worthless since the time I had flunked going into the air force at Plattsburgh years before. I also sensed, and it was also true, that after this one no one in depression-time Wall Street would have me. I was really finished. This was it.

Up to this time I think my drinking had been motivated by the desire for the grandiose. In my cups I fancied, perhaps it was sometimes true, that I could dream great dreams of accomplishment, plan better plans. This terrible urge to [want] distinction and power, prompted by my childhood inferiorities, could be magnified by alcohol. Moreover, I always thought I could see more clearly how the goal could be achieved when in this sort of trance state. Not too much drink, of course, just the right amount. That right amount that all alcoholics would like to be able to drink, to hold that state in which the brain seems [to] be acute, the emotions soar. That had been my motive in drinking thus far.

But now there was a complete and abrupt shift in motivation. I still thought it was the same motivation, but my behavior belied that. I made my way back over to Wall Street, knocking on one inner office door after another but all my friends were so sorry, so sorry. Nothing could be done. Sometimes now I got drunk in the morning even while trying to transact business. When I was crossed, I abused the very people upon whom I was trying to make an impression. Sometimes I had to be led out of offices. When this happened I would repair to the nearest grog shop, throw in a few drinks, buy a bottle, repair to the nearest washroom, and down great quantities. I would try to arrive home not clear out; always concealing a fifth of gin or possibly two. At this point two bottles were far safer. There would be some in the morning. That is, if I could find the one that I hid.

Only briefly now could I dream of the great things to come. These fantasies sped swiftly by. Sometimes my thoughts turned to revenge. How could I get even with this one or that one.

After I got two bottles of gin into the house—I'd do this by leaving them outside and sneaking out for them or hiding them in the lower areaway. One hundred and eighty-two Clinton was a brownstone, and only the dining room and kitchen were in the basement so this made it [a] very convenient place to operate. Besides, like all other alcoholics, I hid liquor about as a squirrel would cherish nuts. Liquor could be found in the attic, on beams, underneath the flooring; it could be found in the flush box of toilets; it could be found buried in coal in the cellar; it could be found in the backyard. I say it could be found—it would be there when my credit was good, when I would take pains during the times when Lois was at work to replenish my stores.

One of the great agonies was to wake up in the morning

not remembering where I had planted a fresh supply the day before.

But to return to my motivation—I now see that I was drinking for oblivion. I either wished to numb my senses or better still, to go altogether. There would be days of drinking about the house, barely able to get through supper, then the blackout. Then a tearful parting with Lois in the morning and at it again for the day. Two and three bottles of gin had become a routine.

This pace was not long in producing frightening hangovers, often bordering on delirium. My morale was utterly shattered. That terrible driving persistence for a goal seemed to have utterly disappeared. All of my conversation was now on the negative side. . . . I was good for nothing. When people tried to counsel with me, even gently, . . . I remember throwing a small sewing machine at poor Lois. At another time I went around through the house kicking out door panels. Seldom had I done anything like this in all my drinking career. Now it was routine when I was bad enough and crossed. In the more lucid times, Lois would tell me, with terror in her eyes, how truly insane I had been. What could we do about it?

Then came the series of remedies that nearly every drinker has tried, when he begins to send for the must-stop-or-else. Lois would give up her job or get a leave of absence and we would go away for months on end. Very often, we went to my brother-in-law's farm in Vermont, at a place called

Green River, near Brattleboro. We'd pitch a tent under some fine old trees out in the pasture. Slowly I would regain my poise. We would tramp the mountains; I would go fishing; we would read for hours on end. The old life ... would begin to come back.

One of my Wall Street friends had sent me a Christian Science practitioner. Though I had not the slightest faith in such business, I went to please him. She gave me Mary Baker Eddy's *Science and Health*. My desperation was so great by now that I used to lie on my stomach in the sun in front of our camping place reading and rereading. Always, I used to say to myself, "Yes, this would work if I could only believe it. But I can't believe." Nevertheless, increasing health and freedom from alcohol would temporarily restore it, but I never

Always, I used to say to myself, "Yes, this would work if I could only believe it. But I can't believe."

recall one of these flights that didn't result in a debacle. In one instance, not long before we were to go back and face the music in New York and had become quite hopeful, I went fishing deep in a high-up notch. The fishing was good. I was utterly sure. I even bordered on being happy. Then I ran across a fisherman. He had a box of sandwiches and he invited me to join him. He sat on a log and I presently saw that he had more than sandwiches. He had a bottle of whiskey.

I can't remember what the rationalization was now, by what excuse I slipped back into insanity. But I arrived home utterly maudlin, having created a scene in the village below.[6]

It was in this period of enforced idleness that I developed the habit of writing when drunk. Until then I hadn't the slightest interest in this art, but I fancied that maybe I could make a living that way.

I remember covering a range of topics. For example, the Roosevelt administration had just come in. The Democrats had campaigned on conservative lines, then came the bank holiday followed by what was to me rank socialistic proposals. After all I had been raised in Republican Vermont.

One evening at a moving picture I saw [Franklin Delano Roosevelt] standing in an automobile, waving his hands in the air over the Wilson Dam at Muscle Shoals, declaring

6. Editor's note—At this point, Bill stops to change the tape, and continues: "I'm in the middle of a narrative about the last two years of my drinking, when I really hit the skids and hit the bottom that made possible my sudden spiritual [awakening]. I guess that part of the narrative . . . relates to the summer of 1933."

that the Tennessee Valley was to become the Ruhr of America, and telling the nation of the marvelous low-cost water power that was to be when the whole river was developed. Having once gone down there to investigate and finding the Wilson Dam nearly dry in the summertime, I had realized the enormous cost per horsepower developing the whole river. Any high school boy could have seen it. So I jumped to the conclusion that FDR was either densely ignorant or must surely be acting in bad faith. This incensed me and I began to write a prophecy about all the perils that would presently beset the Ship of State. The writing would start off with a firm hand, commence to falter, and the ideas would get more diffuse after successive pulls on the gin bottle. . . . At length there would be gibberish and at last trailing scrawls on the paper.

In our upper bedroom on Clinton Street I would sometimes be at this all day. Lois would finally pass it out when she arrived home from the department store and would carefully collect all of this stuff, hiding it or destroying it, for she knew I would be possessed with the notion to put it in a mailbox and ship it to FDR himself. I still wanted to deal with the head man.

But none of these devices could sustain my grandiosity. Forces of destruction gathered in the growing darkness, and little by little my paranoia sank to the bottom of the ego, and depression came on top. Though I seldom admitted it, I guess I really wanted to die. About the only thing that kept me alive was the vestige of responsibility for Lois and the further shame that would be heaped upon her if I took the leap.

At this juncture I had a habit of standing before my father-in-law's medicine cabinet, leaning drunkenly and sizing up the suicide potential that might exist in more forbidding-looking medicine bottles. In part it was a theatrical perfor-mance but in part it was very real. Though this state was almost continuous, there were nevertheless lucid states.

One day at the corner of Broad and Wall Streets I bumped into Clint Frazer, an over-the-counter trader with whom I had a slight acquaintance. Clint told me he was working for a perfectly wonderful Jewish fellow, Joe Hirschhorn, who, despite the times, still had money and was making it hand over fist. I soon met Joe and outlined some of my ideas.

Joe had come up in Wall Street the hard way, starting as a trader in penny stocks when people stood in Broad Street and traded in the curb market. Subsequently his great acu-men had brought him important connections, and he had an uncanny trading flair. Joe was much more of a short-term operator than I had been, but he was nevertheless deeply interested to know the inside situation of companies in which he dealt.

He made me great promises, and I began to be faintly encouraged. Sometimes he would tell me he had bought a line of stock and was carrying me for a few shares on credit. Now and then he would hand me a small check. This was usually spent on fifths of gin, now the delicatessen variety.

On one occasion, though, he handed me a check for twenty-five hundred dollars. This seemed like a terrific sum to have in my hand, and right away I thought of Lois up there at Macy's and, half-tight I made my way into the store and presented her with the check as an example of my returning prowess in the Street. She carried the check home. [Thereafter, I was] well under the weather in the evening. Whereupon I begged the check back, saying that I could rapidly pyramid it into ten times this amount if only I might have it. I think I actually opened a small trading account. The money was promptly lost on a dip in the market [and] on a further plunge into a sea of alcohol.

By now the going was getting pretty rough in Clinton Street, financially speaking. Lois's mother had died in 1930, and her father still hung on there in the agency business, but nearly all of his old patients had passed away and the changing times had greatly impaired his fortunes. . . .

One afternoon I was reeling home, and there I saw the dear old doctor standing on the steps with two or three people. He had just been showing them an apartment. I obligingly fell flat on my face, right in front of the house. I was still conscious a little, and made an effort to go on to the stoop. The lease was canceled on this apartment and excepting the time that I was too drunk in the morning to shovel the snow off the sidewalk in front of the place, this was the only occasion on which the old gentleman got thoroughly angry with me.

No drinker himself, yet he somehow understood, and I have never known why.

Well, it wasn't too bad. Lois and I would fall into long discussions about this thing. Certainly a power greater than myself had me, and that was life with John Barleycorn. We pondered that age-old question for hours: Why couldn't I stop? Day after day I would pledge to be better. Sometimes I would make up my mind to quit entirely, and I would then be in the toils within the hour. I tried to describe to her those queer states of mind which just preceded that first drink that invariably set me off. I seemed unable to remember the terrible consequences of even the last two sprees, and all my pledges and well meanings. These would somehow recede into the recesses of my mind and some trivial rationalization would permit me to get started again.

> Certainly a power greater than myself had me, and that was life with John Barleycorn.

Sometimes, though, there would be a little consciousness of what I was about to do. I would start walking toward the delicatessen store, where I had a credit, for the invariable gin. I would say to myself, "I shouldn't be doing this, but I'm going to do it." Over and over I'd repeat this until I stood before the proprietor. He always knew what I wanted.

Sometimes I would simply be taken drunk, not able in the least to recall the process of mind that preceded that first drink. Most of the time the mental machinery operated as in the time of the Jersey lightning episode, but now it was a continuous performance.

The emotional and physical toll upon Lois and me began to be terrific. First her immense resources of strength, her valor began to fail. The tension and strain laid [waste on] her nervous system. I had become as spent and disjointed as a scarecrow. I could eat little. After an especially severe debauch, it might be two or three days before much of anything would stay in my stomach. These periods of forced diets were always due to the lack of one thing—money.

In utter desperation and terror, I began to steal from Lois's slender purse, and on some occasions I would hock articles filched from the house. The curve of my declining resources had now become a straight line; the place, downward. Isolation and loneliness [were common states of mind]. This wasn't only a mental state, either. None of our friends would have anything to do with us, socially or otherwise.

My mother, after a very successful period as an osteopathic physician, had married a cancer specialist, and they had gone to Florida. And there was practically no contact with my father, who had also remarried, taking up his life in British Columbia, still a quarryman.

Well, there was occasional contact by mail with Mother. I don't believe that in all the years I had seen my father half a dozen times. But even Mother had little idea of the sad estate in which I had fallen.

There were only four people who still stood by. Lois and

her father; my brother-in-law, Leonard Strong; and my sister, Dorothy. Leonard was an osteopathic physician too. They lived at Yonkers then, and he had an office in New York, where he carried on a mighty successful practice. Often he would treat me for terrible hangovers, and we would discuss my affairs.

At length my condition became so frightful that I began to be a regular visitor at Towns Hospital, 293 Central Park West. My visits there began, I think, in the fall of 1933, and though the pledge was pretty expensive, my brother-in-law came to the rescue, aided at the last by my mother, who was then told what the score was.

My first visit to Towns was the occasion for the only hope I had had in months. It was here that I met a little man who was destined for greatness in the annals of Alcoholics Anonymous, Dr. William Duncan Silkworth. As I came out of the fog that first time, I saw him sitting by the bedside. A great, warm current of kindness and understanding seemed to flow out of him. I could deeply feel this at once, though he said scarcely a word. He was very slight of figure and then pushing sixty, I should say. His compassionate blue eyes took me in at a glance, as they peered out of his glasses. A shock of pure white hair gave him a kind of otherworldly look. At once, befuddled as I was, I could sense he knew what ailed me. His first assurance was that I was a sick man, very sick too. He made no bones about that. But, still, he said, I was more sick than sinful. Then in simple words he described the illness. He said my habit of drinking had become an obsession. This condemned me to drink against my will. That I truly wanted to stop, he had no question.

There was another complication also. He said that I had become physically allergic to alcohol, that my body would no longer tolerate it, hence these frightening hangovers and mental deviations. But the nub of the situation was the obsession that condemned me to drink against my will. So the real problem was to break the obsession, to restore my sanity with respect to alcohol.

. . . he just handed me that double-pronged dilemma and let me look at it. Instead of being shocked, I found this news an immense and indescribable relief.

He didn't theorize much, he just handed me that double-pronged dilemma and let me look at it. Instead of being shocked, I found this news an immense and indescribable relief. At last I'd found someone who understood, and I understood myself. It raised the unbearable burden of shame and guilt. It gave me something to point at. My confusion was resolved. The problem was clean-cut, and I rose to the challenge. So long adrift in a rudderless boat, so enveloped in the dark night of the soul, this was like a flashing beacon on the horizon to be reached.

This beacon brightened as my brain cleared. At Towns in those days, they gave one some sedative, an occasional shot of whiskey, which was taken down to nothing in about three days; meanwhile they plied you with castor oil and belladonna. How the world brightened up as my brain began to clear. Only now did I realize how badly I had been benumbed for month, yes, years. Poisoned body, poisoned mind, poisoned emotions. All these were on [the] mend at once. Dawn was coming, and I waited for the sunrise. Graduated to my bathrobe, I ventured to the roof. There was a solarium up there, a pool table, and a lot of gymnastic apparatus. One forenoon I bumped into Charlie Towns, the proprietor. Charlie was one of those American success stories. He had been a poor Georgia farm boy and later, banging around the world, his travels had taken him to China, where he'd seen belladonna applied to opium addicts.

Later he and the celebrated Dr. Lambert, expert on alcoholism and the heart conditions that go with it, had founded the Charles B. Towns Hospital. They began to use belladonna and whatever other stuff. It was called the Lambert Treatment for Alcoholism and Dope Addiction.

Charlie stood about six-one, perfectly proportioned and,

even in advanced years, was a physical prodigy. He radiated an animal vitality that hit people like a ton of bricks. Charlie lectured me, as he apparently did all the others. He was a great believer in gymnastics, spending about two hours a day in the New York Athletic Club himself. He never missed if he could help it.

Well, the subject of his lecture was this: no booze, plenty of exercise with the dumbbells, and muscle up the old willpower. Of course, anybody could stop if they really wanted to, once the poison was taken out of them by the famous Towns-Lambert treatment.

I must say in fairness, though, that Charlie didn't talk too much about curing alcoholism. At one time their literature had used the word, but it had been dropped. Lots of the patients were repeaters, people who had no idea of stopping. These fellows just wanted to be put in shape to drink again.

All of this impedimenta covered Charlie's finer nature, which I was later to see, for he plays an important part in my narrative to come. On this first meeting, though, he did jar me. The spectacle of his success and his vast will to live lustily got me down.

No two people could have been set in greater contrast than he and Dr. Silkworth. Those long talks with that benign little man will be treasured among my dearest possessions unto the end of my days. We used to sit out in the sun in a corner hedged around with plants. During these talks, some of his own stories fell out.

As an M.D. he'd never had even a nodding acquaintance with greatness. As a fact, he wasn't a psychiatrist at all. He was a neurologist. He had acquired, in a small way—he had accumulated a small competence during the 1920s from private practice. In boom times a number of hospitals were built from public stock subscriptions, well watered for the most part. All of the little man's life savings went into one of these, and part of the salestalk carried the promise of a fine post for him on the staff of the hospital-to-be. His dream crashed in the tornado of 1929, and all his worldly goods were lost.

In desperation he made a connection with Towns Hospital, where he was given the grandiose title of chief physician, or physician in chief. The pay was pitiful, something like forty dollars a week and board, I think. His arrival at Towns was the great turning point of his life. This was now the fall of 1933, and he'd arrived in 1930. He told me how, seeing the miserable wreckage that floated through the place, he had resolved to try to do something about it. Even to me he admitted the great hopelessness of the situation so far as most of those afflicted went. But there were certain cases, he said. He glowed as he told me about them. He'd long since forgotten about fame and fortune. What could he do about alcoholism? That was the thing. All those millions with this mysterious malady of mind, emotions, and body.

He'd formed, later, this theory of an allergy. Obviously

there was a lessening tolerance to liquor in all these cases, and the obsession spoke to itself. It screamed on all sides.

I listened to this little man, entranced. God knows I had been surrounded by those who cared and a few who still cared. But this one understood. And he cared, too, in a deep, special way. In his lifetime, the doctor was to talk to fifty thousand cases of alcoholism. But not a one was a case; they were all human beings. He cared for them collectively and, more important, he cared for them severally. Each one was something very special in his book. I instantly perceived this. He had a way of making me feel that my recovery meant everything to him, it mattered so much. Not a great M.D., this man, but a very great human being.

Later an AA friend was to do a stirring piece about him in our monthly magazine, the *Grapevine*. And the title he chose was this, "The Little Doctor Who Loved Drunks." My friend had said it all.[7]

In his lifetime, the doctor was to talk to fifty thousand cases of alcoholism. But not a one was a case; they were all human beings.

As I have said, Silky was neither a theorist nor a psychiatrist. Though he, of course, took a good history of me, my childhood, problems, marriage, and the like, he did not

---

7. Editor's note—At this point, the recording stops, and Bill then begins where he had left off: "This is the day after Labor Day, 1954. Ed and I are back in the Bedford Hotel and we're just about to pick up the narrative where I left off, not finishing my impressions of

engage in any investigation of depth, or at least he never let me know about it if he did. On the face of this record, his summation was that I was a person of rather unusual emotional sensitivity, inclined to childishness and grandiosity, which alternated with depression. But upon my marriage, which has certainly been wondrously happy, save the drinking, the early childhood mood swings had seemed to straighten out. Though I have no doubt that he saw maladjustments and personality deformities in me galore, it was his method never to say this.

It was then his way, and continued to be, to direct people away from a deep and also often morbid examination of the past, the kind that alcoholics get into so often when under psychiatric treatment. He went straight at the problems that were obvious and conscious and let the unconscious take care of itself.

From the psychiatric standpoint, of course, this was the rankest sort of heresy. Nevertheless, the fact remains that the old man had more success with alcoholics, even before AA, than perhaps any individual in the world. In general this

Dr. Silkworth. I will now deal with his presentation of the alcoholic picture to me and the effort he made to transmit his ideas and help me. Ed says this is September the seventh. I must try to keep my voice up, as I am still very tired, though gaining very rapidly under the stimulation of the prospect of going to work again and having someone of Ed's immense vitality, ability, and caliber around. I have been so much alone of late. Let's see how this is recording now; we want to soup it up all we can."

is the method of Alcoholics Anonymous today, as we first present our picture to the newcomer. We take him off the hook on guilt, shame, and morbidity, by charging his behavior up to his illness, truly search it for character defects on a moral basis.

And when I first met Silky, as we affectionately call him, he was doing just that, too, but never with heavy emphasis. Never on the basis of lecturing or sermonizing. Besides, he made a great point of sensing the good in people, on showing how it had been run over and obliterated by this dire malady, the obsession plus the allergy. He had also come to distinguish three states that the alcoholic people who are getting well always pass through. He realized that there was a period of obliquity, of rebellion, of this-can't-be-me-ism, which was a bar to any progress whatever until the candidate got more hurt.

Then he clearly recognized and defined that in-between stage, where the pain is rising more sharply and the patient has periods of wanting to want to stop. Like AA, it was his practice to hurry the alcoholic through this stage by brandishing the awful malignity of the malady, to show that nothing but an utter willingness to do anything could take him out of the toils, even at this uncertain time, when perhaps drinking was momentarily a pleasure.

Then there was the stage that always just antedates recovery, the stage in which the alcoholic is willing to do anything, absolutely anything to get well. He sees the extent of his commitment to alcohol, deeply realizes its gravity, and wishes to be done with it forever. This is what the good old doctor called the point of decision, final and irrevocable decision. Ordinary resolutions or reservations that one might be able to drink in moderation someday, trips on the water-wagon—one by one, he would break up these delusions.

So, in Silky's kit of tools I found two of immense potency and worth, and these were to become his bequests to the society of Alcoholics Anonymous. The first was his rare and immense capacity to somehow engage the utter confidence of alcoholic sufferers. Somehow he could come in and be with us in the caves in which we lived. I never knew anything about his personal sufferings, yet he must have had them. But everyone who knew him understood his immense capacity for love. And love for the isolated, stigmatized alcoholic of 1934 was something pretty rare to find in the medical profession, or indeed, anywhere at all except in the persons of those few devoted ones of a family that still clung to an alcoholic.

. . . love for the isolated, stigmatized alcoholic of 1934 was something pretty rare to find in the medical profession, or indeed, anywhere at all . . .

So the doctor's treatment rested squarely on his ability to make an identification with us alcoholics. One which I suspect ran to great depth.

His second great resource was a constant reiteration of

alcoholism as an illness, an illness of mind and body, neatly packaged in those two words, the allergy plus the obsession.

As I have related, this was a ten-strike [to me], as it has since been to uncounted AA members. It was the absolution of shame and guilt and confusion that left only the obsession to deal with. Not only did it minimize the obsession, but there was the challenge of it. Cleared of poisons by physical treatment, picturing a joyous existence without alcohol, the demon could be attacked and vanquished. To prove this he cited a considerable number of case histories, Galahads newly armored, who had killed the beast for good.

Understanding, decision, hope. These were the instruments that would exorcise this devil.

I left Towns Hospital a new man, or at least so I thought. Though terrifying experiences lay ahead, the foundation for my recovery was already laid, in part. Providence was preparing a table to be set in the presence of our ancient enemy, Barleycorn. And Dr. Silkworth had placed upon it its first candles. Never shall I forget the first courage and joy that surged in me as I opened the door to enter 182 Clinton Street, Brooklyn. I embraced Lois, our union was renewed, her color was so much better, her step elastic. Visiting me each night at the hospital, she had seen my courage and spirit on the mend and she, too, had talked to the doctor. This was it, of that we were both certain.

She had got in flowers for the house. There were all the things that I loved to eat. She rattled on about the wonderful weekends we would soon have. How we'd go camping on the Palisades. Maybe we'd hire a rowboat at Yonkers as we once did. Cut saplings for spars, hoist on these a bath towel, as once upon a time we sailed free before the wind. She'd got together all sorts of games, silly little things. We'd play them again and be happy children. She hadn't overlooked the golf mania either, which still clung to me. She'd bought a little gadget approximating a golf hole, which could be set in the middle of the rug, and we both set at work after supper putting into it. There was a board with a square hole in it, and beanbags. . . .We'd play at that too. Yes, life would begin again and oh, how deeply we both believed it.

. . . I can't recall when I next got drunk again. I don't know whether I remained sober two months or four months. There was a happy interlude, but I suppose the disillusionment of crashing after this short chore was so devastating that I . . . just can't seem to reconstruct it.

At any rate, Lois and I both hit a new emotional low, but again the good doctor came to the rescue, and though more conservative and chastened, I left Towns after the second trip with considerable renewal of hope. He pointed out that several of his cases who had finally achieved success had experienced such episodes, that it was disconcerting, even intensely discouraging, but no bar to recovery if I'd really work for it along the new lines of understanding.

My next relapse occurred, I am sure, in a shorter time after treatment than did the first. Likewise, I can't remember just how this came about. All I remember is that in the ensuing months, the hopelessness broadened and deepened. I was engulfed by it, and so was Lois. Immense exertion to achieve sobriety. I'd work through hangover after hangover, only to last four or five days, or maybe only one or two. In the night hours I was filled with horror, for snaky things infested the dark. Sometimes by day queer images danced on the wall. Lois would nurse me through the hangovers. I'd taper down onto beer, then over to fruit juice. Eating the first real meal was a terrible experience, but I'd feel I had to do it, I was so terribly weak. A day or two later, I might limp over to Wall Street, only to return before noon. Sometimes I'd get almost in the clear, and then suddenly, the first drink.

In this period I was often taken drunk without knowing how or why, something which is unbelievable to many AAs. It was the obsession plus, and the plus stood for insanity. I didn't want to go to Towns again. I couldn't take the doctor. But at length, in midsummer of 1934, I was taken there in terrific shape. I think my brother-in-law, Leonard Strong, was of especial aid on this occasion. I was three or four days regaining any semblance of my faculties. Then depression set in.

One hot summer night, Lois came to see me and afterward had a talk with the doctor. Downstairs, she began to ask him the questions that wives of alcoholics must have posed time out of mind: "How bad is this? Why can't he stop? What's become of the tremendous willpower he once had? Where, oh, where, doctor, are we heading?" And finally, "What's to be done now? Where do we go from here?"

The little man was, of course, used to questions like these. They were asked of him every day, but as he later told me, they always hurt, it was so hard to tell the stark truth. But, in his gentle way, the old man finally told her, "I thought at first that Bill might be one of the exceptions, because of his very great desire to quit, because of his character and intelligence. I thought he might be one of the very few. But his habit of drinking has now turned into an obsession, one much too deep to be overcome, and the physical effect of it on him has also been very severe, for he's showing some signs of brain damage. This is true even though he hasn't been hospitalized very much. Actually I'm fearful for his sanity if he goes on drinking."

"... I'm fearful for his sanity if he goes on drinking."

Then Lois asked, "Just what does this mean, doctor?" And the old man slowly replied, "It means that you will have to confine him, lock him up somewhere if he would remain sane, or even alive. He can't go on this way another year, possibly."

This was my sentence, though neither of them told me in so many words. But I didn't need to be told. In my heart I knew it. This was the end of the line. I became far more frightened and confused and mystified than ever. For long hours I thought over my past life. How and why could I have come to this? There had been much that happened, very much indeed. Save for my drinking, Lois and I had had a wonderful life together. My whole career had teemed with excitement and interest, and yet, here I was, bedeviled with an obsession that condemned me to drink against my will and a bodily sensitivity that guaranteed early insanity at best.

This time I left the hospital really terror stricken. By dint of the greatest vigilance, I stayed sober some weeks. By taking extreme care [not] to expose myself to suggestions of drinking, by going over and over again Dr. Silkworth's advice and admonitions. I kept on steering clear. Gradually the weeks lengthened into months. Little by little I took heart again. I even went to Wall Street and fell into a few small deals that brought home a little cash. The badly shattered confidence of a friend or two over there began to be restored. Things looked better, a lot better.

It was already early November, and I hadn't had a drink since June. This was unheard of. Besides, the fright was getting hazier. I didn't have to exert myself so much to resist. I began to talk to people about alcoholism, and when offered drinks, I would give the information to them as a defense and also as a justification for my former condition. Confidence was growing quite fast now. Armistice Day 1934 rolled around. Lois had to go to the Brooklyn department store where she worked. Wall Street was closed down and I began to wonder what I would do. I thought of golf. I hadn't played in a long time. The family purse was slender, so I suggested to Lois that I might go over to Staten Island, where there was a public course. She couldn't quite conceal her apprehension, but managed to say cheerfully, "Oh, please do, that would be wonderful." I soon crossed on the ferry and found myself seated on the bus beside a man with a flying-target rifle. That brought back memories of that Remington single-shot piece my grandfather had given me when I was eleven years old. We got talking about shooting.

Suddenly a bus behind us collided with the one we were in. There wasn't any great shock, neither too much damage. My friend and I alighted on the pavement to wait for the next one to come along. Still talking about shooting irons, we noticed something that looked like a speakeasy. He said to me, "What about a little nip?" I said to him, "Fine, let's go." We walked into the place. He ordered a Scotch, and with ease, I ordered ginger ale. "Don't you drink?" he said.

"No," I said, "I'm one of those people who can't manage it."
And then I dwelt on the allergy and the obsession, etc. I
told him all about the terrible time I'd had with liquor and
how I was through with it forever. Very carefully I explained
the whole illness to him.

Soon, seated in another bus, we were presently deposited in
front of a country inn quite well down the island. I was to go
to the golf course nearby, he was to take another bus to the
rifle range. But it was noontime, so again, he said, "Let's go
in and have a sandwich. Besides, I'd like to have a drink." We
sat at the bar this time. As I have said, it was Armistice Day.
The place was filling up, and so were the customers. That
familiar buzz which rises from drinking crowds filled the
room. My friend and I continued our talk, still on the subject
of shooting. Sandwiches
and ginger ale for me, *My friend looked at me aghast.*
sandwiches and another
drink for him.

We were almost ready to leave when my mind turned
back again to Armistice Day in France, all the ecstasy of
those hours. I remembered how we'd all gone to town. I no
longer heard what my friend was saying. Suddenly the bar-
tender, a big, florid Irishman, came abreast of us, beaming.
In each hand he held a drink. "Have one on the house,
boys," he cried, "It's Armistice Day." Without an instant's
hesitation I picked up the liquor and drank it. My friend
looked at me aghast. "My God, is it possible that you could

take a drink after what you just told me? You must be crazy."
And my only reply could be this, "Yes, I am."[8]

During the next few days I made a frantic effort to sober
up. Sometimes I would almost make it, but to my horror I
found I simply could not. Presently I lapsed into my usual
routine, two to three bottles of bathtub gin a day, drinking
while Lois was at work, going to bed stupefied each night,
in the early forenoons scribbling insane notes to all sorts of
people, lying on the bed, passing out, waking up, and so
things went on for two or three weeks. I vaguely remember
how Lois and I used to discuss this awful dilemma, but
being so befogged, I cannot today recall anything of what
we said. We just lived on, a day at a time, all hope gone.

"You must be crazy." And my only reply
could be this, "Yes, I am."

---

8. Editor's note—At this point in the story, Bill stops the tape and
   resumes at a later time: "Ed and I are at the Bedford Hotel. This is
   Thursday, September 9, 1954. Yesterday I left off at the beginning of
   my last debauch. I want to test this recording."

One afternoon I sat at the kitchen table down in the basement, alone in the house. Considering the time of day, I was fairly lucid. The telephone rang. My old school friend, Ebby Thacher was on the wire. We had met at Burr and Burton, where his parents, prominent Albany people who had summered in Manchester, had sent him for a year on the theory that he would get into less trouble. I had occasionally run into him since, passing through Albany on business trips. I would drop off, and we would make a night of it together.

In early '29, I remember stopping to see Ebby, and he had made the acquaintance of some flying folks. We had had an all-night party and then chartered a plane and pilot to fly from Albany to Manchester, Vermont. They were working on a landing field up there, but no planes had appeared. And we called Manchester to tell the folks that we would be the first arrivals. Tight as he was, the pilot was pretty reluctant, but finally off we went. I vaguely remember spotting the town of Bennington through the haze. The excited citizens of Manchester had got together a welcoming committee. The town band had turned out. The down delegation was headed by Mrs. [Anne] Orvis, a rather stately and dignified lady at that time, who owned the famous Equinox House.

We circled the field, but meantime all three of us had been pulling at a bottle of liquor, cached in the rear cockpit to the front. Somehow we lit on the pretty bumpy meadow. The delegation charged forward. It was up to Ebby and I to do something, but we could do absolutely nothing. We somehow slid out of the cockpit, fell on the ground, and there we lay immobile. Such was the history-making episode of the first airplane ever to alight at Manchester, Vermont.

After a time I found myself at the home of my old friend the postman. The next day, a frightful hangover, a crying jag, in which I wandered all over East Dorset. Then a letter of abject apology to Mrs. Orvis. Now and then I have since heard of Ebby, and the news was all bad. I recognized that he was an alcoholic, going to pieces even faster than I. I had heard that he raised such ructions at Manchester, where he would come in the fall to the family summer house after the rest had returned to the city, that the citizens, though they loved him, had decided to do something about it.

The rumor was that he had been committed to Brattleboro Asylum, one of the state's mental institutions. And yet, this was Ebby on the other end of the phone, and no mistake. Moreover, he was obviously sober. I'd never known of his being in New York sober. My spirits rose, for my gin supply happened to be good just then. Dear old Ebby, I'd soon see him. We'd sit at the kitchen table. Ah, we'd talk about the good old days.

A significant thought this was. There was a good reason for it. We'd talk about the good old days because the present was unbearable and there was to be no future.[9]

9. Editor's note—Bill stops his dialogue to change the tape, which was side 1 of record 6. He speaks through side 2 of record 6, and he decides not to use that material. He then starts record 7: "This is the

Meanwhile, Providence had been preparing a table in the presence of our ancient enemy, Barleycorn. People and forces had been at work, strange events had begun to flow that would one day converge and form Alcoholics Anonymous.

A well-known American businessman named Rowland Hazard had gone to Zurich, Switzerland, probably in the year 1930. Of a fine and wealthy Rhode Island family, he had carried on its social and business tradition; that is, he carried on until alcohol caught up with him. Indeed, I believe he had gone so far as to become a director of one of the great American chemical combines—Allied Chemical. By the late 1920s though, he had been incapable of work because of his prolonged sprees. He had run into all his social and business rebuffs, which we alcoholics know so well. He began the round of psychiatrists, institutions, and cures.

By the time he resolved on the trip to Zurich, his confidence had pretty well waned. Indeed, he was visiting Zurich

Hotel Bedford, September 1954, and this will be record 7. Side 2 of record 6 is to be ignored. I don't think I told the Ebby story very well, so we'll go on from here."

as the court of last resort, for here he was to meet the celebrated Dr. Carl Jung, one of the fathers of modern psychiatry. If this great physician couldn't straighten him out, who could? Rowland Hazard remained with Dr. Jung a whole year; desperately wanting to resolve his problem, he gave fullest cooperation. As the months passed, he began to believe himself cured. His defected personality structure was uncovered as never before. The hidden springs and warped motors of his unconscious mind stood starkly revealed. Fortified by this understanding, Rowland truly believed that he now had a basis upon which to get well.

At the end of twelve months' treatment, he left the doctor to face the world. Thoroughly understanding himself and thoroughly on guard, he could hardly fail, he thought. Yet in a matter of weeks, he got drunk, unaccountably drunk. Frightened, he tried to fight off the compulsion, but alcohol soon had his old way with him. Rowland returned to Dr. Jung in utter despair. Understanding, high resolution, and vigilance hadn't done the job. "What now?" he thought.

. . . he was visiting Zurich as the court of last resort . . .

So he asked the good doctor and got a reply that was to make AA history. The doctor, it appeared, at first thought Rowland one of those rare cases capable of recovery. But before the end of the treatment period, he clearly saw this would probably not be the case, so he now told Rowland point-blank that he had never seen one single alcoholic situation as difficult and grave as Rowland's that had ever made a recovery under his treatment. Dr. Jung humbly confessed that he had poor success with alcoholics, that he was capable of doing nothing whatever for Rowland.

His last prop knocked out, Rowland knew the alcoholic's ultimate despair. As today's AAs would say, he hit bottom, and he hit it hard. This is incredible, he thought. Could there be no hope at all? Was there no other resource anywhere? Then Carl Jung made another statement—the one which saved Rowland Hazard's life and set Alcoholics Anonymous in motion. He said, in effect, "Occasionally, Rowland, alcoholics have recovered through spiritual experiences, better known as religious conversions."

Brightening a little, Rowland rejoined, "But, doctor, you know I am a religious man. I used to be a vestryman of the Episcopal Church."

Carl Jung shook his head. "No, Rowland, that isn't enough. Faith and good works are good, very good. But by themselves they almost never budge an alcoholic compulsion like yours. I'm talking about the kind of religious experience that reaches into the depths of a man, that changes his whole motivation and outlook and so transforms his life that the impossible becomes possible."

"Well, doctor," queried Rowland, "if I must have such an experience, where and how do I find it?"

Said Dr. Jung, "That's something I can't tell you. All you can do is place yourself in a religious atmosphere of your own choosing, admit your personal powerlessness to go on living. If under such conditions you seek with all your might, you may then find. But the experience you need is only occasional; here and there, now and then, alcoholics have recovered through them. You can only try."

Setting out upon his uncertain quest, Rowland presently fell in with the Oxford Groups [OG]. This was a nondenominational evangelical movement, streamlined for the modern world and then at the height of its very considerable success. It had been founded ten or a dozen years earlier by a Lutheran minister, Dr. Frank Buchman. Among his first converts had been an Episcopal clergyman, Dr. Sam Shoemaker, and still another clergyman called Sherry Day. Their aim was to bring the very sort of experience Dr. Jung had described to Rowland. From the beginning they felt their movement had to cross all lines of race, creed, and conditions. So they would deal in simple religious common denominators of all religions which would be potent enough to change the lives of men and women.

They had hoped to set up a chain reaction—one person carrying the good news to the next. Their aim was world conversion. Everybody, as they put it, "needed changing." They had made their first effort upon the Princeton campus among students. With crusading eagerness they pressed their ideas. They set standards for personal conduct which they named as Absolute Honesty, Absolute Purity, Absolute Unselfishness, and Absolute Love.

Agreeing with James in the New Testament, they thought people ought to confess their sins "one to another." Heavily emphasizing this wholesale sort of personal housecleaning, they called the process "sharing." Not only were things to be confessed; something was to be done about them. This something usually took the form of what they called restitution, the restoration of good personal relationships by making amends for harms done.

> Not only were things to be confessed; something was to be done about them. This something usually took the form of what they called restitution . . .

They were most ardent, too, in their practice of meditation and prayer, at least one hour a day, and two hours would be better. They felt that when people commenced to adhere to these high moral standards, continue to share and to make restitution for their sins, and devoted themselves to meditation and prayer, then God could enter and direct their lives. Under these conditions every individual could receive specific guidance which could inspire every decision and act of living, great or small.

Following meditation and prayer they practiced what they call a quiet time, asking God [for] specific directives. Pencil in hand, they wrote down what came to their minds; one could do this alone, with his family, or in the company of a like-minded group which was called a team. Such a way of life was urged upon all comers. It was a very dynamic and sometimes a very aggressive Evangel[ism].

This was a very stiff dose for the Princeton campus; it was also a stiff dose for the Princeton faculty, especially the theological department. At first this approach naturally attracted only students having severe personal problems. Too indiscriminate discussion of these, especially the intimate ones, brought a reaction of alarm from the faculty and loud guffaws from the student body. After a while Frank and associates folded up their tent and moved to the campus of Oxford University in England. More experienced now and happening to run across people ready for this approach who were perhaps more in an emotional balance, they began to succeed. As momentum gathered, they began to get a good press. Up until this time, probably the early '20s, the movement went under the name of Buchmanism. The budding society turned its eyes toward South Africa, where the Boers and English were feuding as of old.

Frank and a number of students made a journey down there, and actually, at least for the time being, did a great deal to compose these differences. South Africa took fire with the idea, and newspaper reporters began to call the movement the Oxford Groups, as they had stemmed from the campus of that university in England.

Progress, thereafter, in the British Isles was rapid. It spread to Norway, to the Low Countries. In America Sam Shoemaker, rector of the Calvary Episcopal Church in New York, set a fast pace.

By the time that Rowland Hazard turned up among these good folk in 1931, the Oxford Groups had begun to get worldwide attention. People in every level of society were interested; they seemed to be able to cross denominational and social lines with ease. The enthusiasm and actual power of the society was immense. Into it Rowland plunged, and to his surprise and joy, his excessive drink promptly left him. He devoted nearly all his time to work and busily carried its gospel to his friends.

The Oxford Groups had made some progress with other alcoholics too. In the New York society, there was a nucleus of what appeared to be several good recoveries. Among those bearing on our story was one Cebra Graves, son of a

Bennington, Vermont, judge. Another was Shep Cornell, one-time playboy and now married to a splendid and well-known socialite, Lee Cornell.

In August of 1934 these alcoholics and their wives foregathered at Rowland Hazard's summer home at Glastonbury, near Bennington, Vermont.

Cebra Graves knew my friend, Ebby, quite well. The Thachers had a summer home in Manchester, where Ebby had become a terrific problem to all the townspeople. His latest exploit had been to run his father's new Packard off the road and into the side of a house, where, plunging into a kitchen, he stepped out very drunk and utterly unharmed, demanding a cup of coffee from the startled occupants. This was the payoff. The town of Manchester saw something had to be done.

So Ebby was brought to heal before Judge Graves, father of Cebra, in his Bennington courtroom. The townsfolk of Manchester demanded his commitment to Brattleboro Asylum. Awaiting the final hearing, Ebby lay drunk in Manchester. So the trio sojourning at Hazard's place determined to make a project of it. Cebra went to his father and asked that Ebby be paroled in his care. The commitment proceedings were temporarily set aside, and Ebby was brought from Manchester to Hazard's place.

Here the embryo of the AA grew some more. Three alcoholics, all of them released from their drink by spiritual process, were talking to a fourth. Of the three, Hazard's case impressed Ebby the most. It was the most desperate—the most like his own. Besides, Ebby learned what science in the person of the great Jung really thought about the chances for recovery that alcoholics had. This, of course, consolidated his condition that he would not get over drinking by himself or by any resource of psychology or psychiatry. So, on the one hand, his hopelessness was stark; on the other, here were three people who were obviously well, happy, and minus the drink obsession.

Then, rather irked by their evangelistic ardor, Ebby listened [not] much more than half willing. Whether he liked it or not, this was obviously his only escape hatch, and he resolved to try to climb out of it. So he shared his sins in detail, braced himself to make restitution to those he'd hurt, participated in the long quiet times, and with much reluctance actually

> . . . with much reluctance [he] actually tried to pray. He began to feel better—a lot better.

tried to pray. He began to feel better—a lot better. The terrible hangover he had been accumulating for months disappeared fast. Maybe this was it, he thought.

Cebra and Shep then brought Ebby to New York. As he didn't have a cent, they lodged him in Calvary's mission over on the East Side. In former years this had been a sort of standard Bowery mission operation—just another good work of the church, but now it was being infiltrated with the Oxford Group ideas and emphasis.

Ebby began to attend meetings at Calvary House and in the body of the church where Sam and scores of eager Oxford Groupers were holding force. What they had presently laid ahold of him. He soon realized he was no longer fighting alcohol; he was released from it. It was an entirely new experience. He'd found friendship and fellowship of a kind he had never known. Maybe this would lead to a decent job, maybe back to the girl who had refused to marry him because of his drink.

Although he still found himself unable to agree with all of the Oxford Group's ideas and attitudes, he felt mightily grateful for what he had received. Then he thought of me.

The areaway bell at 182 Clinton Street rung, and there he stood. I could instantly sense that somehow he was different. Inside we sat at the kitchen table. On it stood a big pitcher of gin and pineapple juice. I put in the pineapple juice with the notion that Lois would be less disturbed on her return home if she found we weren't drinking straight gin. I pushed the pitcher and a glass toward Ebby. He grinned and shook his head. I was dumbfounded; I'd never known him to be in New York sober before. When I pressed him, he said, "No, thanks, not now."

I said, "What? You don't mean to say you're on the wagon?"

"No," he replied, "I wouldn't say I'm on the wagon; I'm just not drinking now." This was both a disappointment and a relief; I'd looked forward to a delirious talk about the old days, but with Ebby sober that wouldn't be so much fun. Nevertheless, there would be more gin left for me next morning when I would really need it.

So there was some small talk, but my curiosity got the better of me. I finally asked, "Ebby, what on earth has got into you? What's this all about?"

With a half smile, he looked straight at me and said, very simply, "I've got religion." He might as well as hit me in the face with a wet mop. I knew they had planned to bug him at Brattleboro Asylum in Vermont; maybe alcoholic insanity had turned into religious insanity. Nevertheless I had to be polite.

So, after a pause, I ventured, "Well, Ebby, what kind of religion is this? What brand have you got?"

"Well," said he, "I don't know that you'd call it *religion*. Maybe that's the wrong word. But late last summer I met up with a group of people who showed me a way out; maybe you'd like to hear about it."

Ebby well knew my prejudices. He knew that my god was science; so carefully avoiding those aspects of the Oxford Group approach that'd disturb me, he told his story. He recounted the simple principles upon which he was trying to work, especially emphasizing the idea that he'd been hopeless. He told how he had got honest about himself and his defects, how he'd been making restitution where it was owed, how he'd tried to practice a brand of giving that demanded no return for himself. Then very dangerly [*sic*] he touched upon the subject of prayer and God. He frankly said he expected me to balk at these notions. Yet when in his distress he had tried, even experimentally, the result had been immediate. Not only had he been released from his desire to drink—something very different from being on the water wagon—he'd found peace of mind and happiness, the like of which he hadn't known for years.

Such was the substance of Ebby's tale as he told it over the kitchen table. He didn't press. He didn't evangelize. He just told a story. Neither did he stay overlong. He left, saying he'd be back anytime I'd like to see him. Again, one alcoholic had been talking to another and that was it. I was already hit far harder than I knew. At first I reflected he hadn't given me a single new idea. I knew I was hopeless; besides, Dr. Silkworth had said so.

> . . . one alcoholic had been talking to another and that was it. I was already hit far harder than I knew.

Surely, there wasn't anything original in trying to be more honest, loving, pure, and unselfish. Nor was the notion of confession or restitution novel, or of trying to help other people for the joy of it. Yet I soon found that what he said stuck.[10]

10. Editor's note—Bill stops to change the tape, and he reviews where he has left off: "This is side 2 of record 7. Ebby has just left Clinton Street after his first visit, and I am just starting to think over what he told me. The good of what he said stuck so well that in no

Lois came home, and we talked late. At times I felt rather excited and both of us began to use a word we had forgotten. That word was *hope*. However, I kept on drinking, but now more restrained. While Lois was at work, I would sit all day long in the kitchen, the bottle on the table, thinking.

Up to a point Ebby had made plenty of sense. Confession and restitution might be difficult. The pace he set was certainly fast. But how was I to swallow this garbage? I'd had one of those modern educations and had learned that man is god, the spearhead of evolution. What was he talking about, anyway?

Then I would go over on the other tack. After all, he was sober and I was drunk. Who was crazy? Maybe it was me. And so I would seesaw from hope to rebellion and back again. One afternoon Ebby turned up with a friend, Shep Cornell. He'd been a drinker too. Now near the top echelon of the Oxford Groups, he didn't seem to be much like Ebby at all. When he told about his drinking I thought he was a sissy. Just an episode boy, hadn't really suffered much. He soon let me see that he was a socialite, and I didn't like socialites.

He gave me the Oxford Group's boast, aggressively and with all the punch he could pack. I didn't like this at all. When they were gone I took to the bottle and really punished it. But the mood swings went on, rebellion to hope

waking moment thereafter could I get that man and his message out of my head."

135

and back again. Pretty maudlin one day, I got a great idea. I'd figured it was time I did some investigation on my own hook. Remembering the mission where Ebby stayed, I figured I'd go and see what did they do, anyway, down there. I'd find out.

I left the subway at Fourth Avenue and Twenty-third Street. It was a good long walk across Twenty-third, so I began stopping in bars. This consumed most of the afternoon, and I forgot all about the mission. At nightfall I found myself in an excited conversation with a Finn named Alec. He said he'd been a sailmaker in the old country, and a fisherman too. Somehow that word *fisherman* clicked. I thought again of the mission. Over there I would find fishers of men. It seemed like a wonderful idea.

I put persuasion on Alec, and soon we reeled in the front door. Tex Francisco, an ex-drunk in charge, was right there to meet us. He not only ran the mission; he proposed to run us out of it. This made us very sore, when we thought of our good intentions.

Just then Ebby turned up, grinning like a Cheshire cat. He said, "What about a plate of beans?" After the beans, Alec and I were both clearer. Ebby said that there would be a meeting in the mission pretty soon. Would we like to come? Sure, we'd go. That's why we were there. The three of us were soon sitting on one of the hard wooden benches that filled the place. I shivered a little as I looked at the derelict audience. I could smell sweat and alcohol. What the suffering was I pretty well knew.

There were hymns and prayers. Tex, the leader, exhorted us. Only Jesus could save, he said. Certain men got up and made testimonials. Numb as I was, I felt interest and excitement rising. Then came the call. Penitents started marching forward to the rail. Unaccountably impelled, I started too, dragging Alec with me. Ebby reached for my coattails, but it was too late.

Soon I knelt among the sweating, stinking penitents. Maybe then and there, for the very first time, I was penitent too. Something touched me. I guess it was more than that. I was hit. I felt a wild impulse to talk. Jumping to my feet, I began.

Afterward, I could never remember what I said. I only know that I was in earnest, and people seemed to pay attention. Afterward, Ebby, who had been scared to death, told me with relief that I had done all right and had given my life to God.

> . . . I could never remember what I said. I only know that I was in earnest, and people seemed to pay attention.

Upstairs, after the meeting, I saw the dormitories where the penitents slept. I met a few who made a recovery. Some were living at the mission, working outside by day. Eagerly I listened to their stories. I sobered up very fast, and the dead weight on me seemed to go on lifting. With a qualm, I remembered Lois. I hadn't phoned her. She'd be worried. I must tell her all about this.

It was good to hear her sigh of relief at the other end of the wire. Slowly and quite confidently I made my way up Twenty-third Street to the subway. As I went down the stairs it startled me to realize I hadn't thought of looking in at any of the bars.

Before bed, Lois and I had a long talk. Now here was hope in every word. I slept as a child, without an ounce of gin. Due for a terrible hangover the next morning, there was little at all, but that small hangover was my undoing once more. Though I was pretty sure I'd seen some daylight, I felt I would be more comfortable watching the sun come up if I had a drink—one or two, maybe. Saying nothing to Lois, I took aboard a couple, and followed them up with Listerine. She noticed nothing and I felt fine.

After she left for work, the hangover got troublesome again. This was to be the last one. I felt justified in tapering off so, as usual, I tapered up instead of off, and at six o'clock the poor girl found me upstairs on the bed, dead drunk.

But I had seen some light, and there was more to come as events soon revealed. To the best of my recollection, I drank on for another two or three days. But I kept pondering that mission experience. Sometimes it seemed real. Then again I would brush it away, charge it off to an alcohol-fired imagination.

But on the morning of the third day my wandering thoughts gathered into a sharp focus. I remember comparing myself to a cancer victim. Were I such a one, I would do anything to get well, wouldn't I? Anything whatever. Would I sit home rubbing Pond's Extract on the wound? No, of course not. What would I do? Well, I'd head for the best physician in the business and beg him to destroy or cut away those consuming cells. That's what I'd do. I would have to depend on him, my god of medicine, to save me. My dependence would be absolute. For myself I could do nothing.

But alcoholism is my illness, not cancer. Yet what was the difference? Was not alcoholism also a consumer of body and mind? And perhaps, if one had such a thing, of soul. Alcoholism took longer to kill, but the result was the same. Yes, if there was any great physician that could cure the alcohol sickness, I'd better seek him now, at once. I'd better find what my friend had found. Was I like the cancer sufferer who would do anything to get well? If getting well required me to pray at high noon in the public square with the other sufferers, would I swallow my pride and do that? Maybe I would. Meanwhile, though, I'd better get straight over to the hospital, where Dr. Silkworth would thoroughly sober me up again. Then I could look clear-eyed at my friend's formula. Perhaps I wouldn't need an emotional conversion. After all, a conservative atheist like me ought to be able to get on without anything like that! Anyhow, I'd better start for the hospital and right now.

Walking up Clinton Street to the subway, I fished six cents out of my pocket. Never mind, I thought, a nickel would get me to the hospital. But hadn't I forgotten something? Here

I was on my way to be cured. I might as well be comfortable until the hospital took over. So I stepped into a grocery store where I had a slim credit. I remember explaining to the clerk that I was an alcoholic on my way to be cured. Nevertheless, could I have four bottles of beer on the cuff?

I drank one of these on the street and another in the subway. My spirits rose as I offered the third to a passenger. I felt surprised when he turned my refreshment down. So I swallowed that bottle on the station platform near the hospital. Holding the last bottle by its neck I walked into Towns Hospital where Dr. Silkworth met me in the hall.

Now in very high spirits, I waved the bottle and shouted, "At last, Doc, I've found something!" Even through my haze I could see the good old man's face fall. I now know how much he really loved me. This fresh outburst really hurt him. I tried to explain the new thing I thought I'd found. Still he continued to look at me, shaking his head. After a while he quietly said, "Well, my boy, isn't it time you got upstairs and got to bed?"

Without the usual arguments, I meekly did just that. The usual treatment began. Barbiturates to temper me down, doses of belladonna, and a little sedative. I wasn't in such bad shape this time, for it would have taken me another sixty days of hard drinking to bring me to the verge of delirium tremens. So I began to clear up quite rapidly.

But the clearer I got, the more my spirits fell. I began to be frightfully depressed, and Lois came to see me each night after work, looking so sad and sick. The depression would become appalling after she left. I . . . collapsed. Maybe it would be a good thing if I died.

Cold sober now, the god Ebby had talked about seemed improbable, unreal. I could accept all his ideas save this. Briefly, I went on rebelling. My depression deepened, deepened. It gripped me in a living death.

One morning, the fourteenth of December, I think, Ebby appeared in the doorway of my room looking the picture of health and confidence. Sympathy and understanding mingled with his smile as he said, "Mighty sorry you had to land up here again. Thought I'd come up and say hello." As he started to talk, I felt better. What he said at this point I don't remember, but I did notice that he pointedly avoided the topics of alcohol and religion. He was just paying a friendly visit, asking for nothing. He wasn't going to try any evangelism on me after all.

> Cold sober now, the god Ebby had talked about seemed improbable, unreal.

This inspired me to start asking questions myself. Then he began to repeat his pat little formula for getting over drinking. Briefly and without ado he did so. Again he told how he found he couldn't run his own life, how he got honest with himself as never before. How he'd been making amends to the people he'd damaged. How he'd been trying to give of himself without putting a price tag on his

efforts, and finally how he'd tried prayer just as an experi-
ment and had found to his surprise that it worked.

Once more he emphasized the difference between being
on the water wagon and his present state. He no longer had
to fight the desire to drink. The desire had been lifted right
out of him. It had simply vanished. He no longer sat on a
powder keg. He was released. He was free. That was his
simple story.

After I asked a few more questions he turned the talk to
other matters. After a bit he left, promising to return soon
again.

While Ebby talked I had almost surfaced from my
depression, but the only conflict soon renewed itself. Had
Ebby recovered through reality or by an illusion? Who or
what was this god that so many people were so sure of?
What made them so sure that this . . . sad and fathomless
face among a million of suns was so darned important? The
great forces of the cosmos responded to laws, some of
which were known. But laws for what, or for whom? And
did these laws have an author? That life on all levels was so
cruelly competitive, so seemingly pointless. Men died and
more were born. Cats ate birds, birds ate bugs, but dodo
birds had gone extinct, and so had hundreds of other
species, and all for what? Law here, chaos there. Sense
here, nonsense there. . . . People talked about just loving a
person. On the face of it that had to be nonsense. I simply
couldn't go for it. I just wasn't capable of such an absurd

illusion, even though it might save my life for a little while longer.

Depression caught me again. The undertow was remorseless and I sank.[11]

One scene after another crossed through my mind as the depression grew. I thought of Lois, how magnificent, how devoted, how unwavering she had been. Fair weather or foul, it had always been the same. Never had she failed me. I remembered our marriage in Swedenborgian Church in Brooklyn. Our first tiny apartment in New Bedford, Massachusetts. Our first foray there into high society, how joyful that had been. As for drinking, there had been a humiliating episode or so, but this was only a cloud on the horizon no larger than a man's hand. Again we stood together on the cliffs at Newport, knowing I'd sail for World War I soon. Would this be the beginning of our lives together, or the end of it all?

11. Editor's note—Bill stops here to change the tape, and resumes: "This is the Hotel Bedford, September 27, 1954. It is record 8, side 1, and I am about now to tell of my spiritual experience, the great event that transformed my life. So here goes."

I remembered, but could no longer feel, the ecstasy of sacrifice that we shared there. There was a power greater than ourselves, and that was America. She had to come first. I remembered how I had tested a new dimension of life, first in the hold of the *Lancashire,* and then at Winchester Cathedral.

The war was over and I caught a sight of her again on the docks of Hoboken. Hope, confidence, and love, all these we had in great measure. Memories of the exciting struggle for success in greater than fearsome New York City returned.

Ruefully I recalled how the alcohol cloud had spread clear across the horizon, inexplicable, mysterious. How subtle fears of the night to come occasionally beset us. I thought how we had drawn closer together as the menace grew nearer. The stratagem we had tried, the escape to the country. Even that day we had hired a rowboat at Yonkers, loaded it with camping gear, had heisted the bath towel as a sail, and running free before the wind, had reached the Palisades.

Then the crash of 1929 had descended in the night. Always, Lois was there, and even now she was beside me, hiding her hopelessness and waiting. Waiting for what? Well, we both knew. We were waiting for the end. All that mattered was past and gone. Shame and failure had replaced success, and fear had banished security. Of romance there would be none, for presently I would die or go mad. This was the finish, the jumping-off place.

The terrifying darkness had become complete. In agony of spirit, I again thought of the cancer of alcoholism which had now consumed me in mind and spirit, and soon the body. But what of the Great Physician? For a brief moment, I suppose, the last trace of my obstinacy was crushed out as the abyss yawned.

I remember saying to myself, "I'll do anything, anything at all. If there be a Great Physician, I'll call on him." Then, with neither faith nor hope I cried out, "If there be a God, let him show himself." The effect was instant, electric. Suddenly my room blazed with an indescribably white light. I was seized with an ecstasy beyond description. I have no words for this. Every joy I had known was pale by comparison. The light, the ecstasy. I was conscious of nothing else for a time.

The terrifying darkness had become complete.

Then, seen in the mind's eye, there was a mountain. I stood upon its summit where a great wind blew. A wind, not of air, but of spirit. In great, clean strength it blew right through me. Then came the blazing thought, "You are a free man." I know not at all how long I remained in this state, but finally the light and the ecstasy subsided. I again saw the wall of my room. As I became more quiet a great peace stole over me, and this was accompanied by a sensation difficult to describe. I became acutely conscious of a presence which seemed like a veritable sea of living spirit. I lay on the shores of a new world. "This," I thought, "must be the great reality. The God of the preachers."

Savoring my new world, I remained in this state for a long time. I seemed to be possessed by the absolute, and the curious conviction deepened that no matter how wrong things seemed to be, there would be no question of the ultimate rightness of God's universe. For the first time I felt that I really belonged. I knew that I was loved and could love in return. I thanked my God who had given me a glimpse of His absolute Self. Even though a pilgrim upon an uncertain highway, I need be concerned no more, for I had glimpsed the great beyond.

Save a brief hour of doubt next to come, these feelings and convictions, no matter what the vicissitude, have never deserted me since. For a reason that I cannot begin to comprehend, this great and sudden gift of grace has always been mine.

As the wonder of all this deepened, I tried to analyze its meaning. Clergymen had always said to me, "Have faith and then you will be free." Psychologists and psychiatrists had said, "Understand yourself and that will liberate you." Sociologists had said, "Change your environment, and your personality will again flower." But somehow none of these formulas had worked. I'd been incapable of faith and so, God's help. The more I analyzed myself, the worse I got, and my whole life had been a struggle to get to what I thought would be a better environment. Yet, out of no faith, faith had suddenly appeared. No blind faith either, for it was fortified by the consciousness of the presence of God. Despair had turned into utter security. Darkness was banished by cosmic light. For sure I'd been born again. But how, and why?

Despite these wonderful feelings and reflections, I did though, have my hour of doubt. Briefly, I panicked. My scientific education asserted itself. It told me that I was hallucinating, that this just couldn't be so. As this thought bored into me, I became much frightened. Maybe I'd better call Dr. Silkworth. He'd be honest with me. Besides he was a good alienist, an expert on mental aberrations.

Soon he was sitting by my bed, peering at me intently. Somewhat consciously I told him the story of what had happened. It was all so incredible that I still feared to give him the full impact of it. But the essential facts, toned down somewhat emotionally, I did relate to him. Obviously fascinated, he plied me with questions. Point-blank I finally asked him the one that nagged me. "Doctor, is this real? Am I still perfectly sane?"

Then came his reply. Words which were to make AA history. Said he, "Yes, my boy, you were sane, perfectly sane in my judgment. You have been the subject of some great psychic occurrence, something that I don't understand. I've read of these things in books, but I've never seen one myself before. You have had some kind of conversion experience. I'm a man of science and don't pretend to understand these things at all, but I know they do happen and they sometimes cure alcoholics. While I can't put my finger on the reason, I do know that something tremendous has happened to you. You are already a different individual. So, my boy, whatever you've got now you'd better hold on to. It's so much better than what had you only a couple of hours ago."

So spoke the man of science and medicine, but far more importantly, so spoke a very great human being.

The deep faith that she and the little doctor showed in my recovery was all that I needed.

Lois came that evening. I'd hardly begun my tale before she, too, knew that I was well. To this day she has never been able to explain her sudden conviction. As she often says, "Right away I knew it, I knew it." The deep faith that she and the little doctor showed in my recovery was all that I needed. Thus ended the greatest day that I shall ever know.

On waking next morning, I found that my thoughts and feelings had not changed a particle. I was still in the new world, the universe that now made sense. I was at peace with myself and all men. I felt free. I was surrounded and, indeed, filled with that life-giving presence which had made my assurance that all was so well so complete.

All day long my mind centered upon this miracle, this strange and mysterious gift. I had been no better and probably no worse than a million other alcoholics. Why had this happened to me? And why, among the great mass of sufferers in all the time that men had used alcohol, hadn't this happened to any of them? Certainly I had done nothing to earn this gift, but perhaps, quite unwillingly, I had met certain conditions and made the gift possible. Perhaps there had been other factors or forces that worked outside of myself. Then I thought of the terrific impression my friend Ebby had made on me. Despite my cry of rebellion, clearly enough his impact had been deeper than I first realized. Why had he been so successful when others had failed? In Lois and in the successful career that had been promised, there had been plenty of incentive to get well. Dr. Silkworth had given me great understanding and secured my entire confidence. My father-in-law, Dr. Burnham, had tried hard, but to no avail. So had lots of other people with great good-will.

Then, along comes Ebby and in a couple of brief talks, he somehow prepares me for release into a new life. On the third day, Ebby turned up with a book in his hand. As I gave an account of my crashing experience, he seemed a little nonplussed. He'd seen no bright lights, nor had he stood on a high mountain.

Yet, as we compared notes, it became evident that the end products of his experience were the same. He felt he'd found a new dimension of life, and he carried the same feeling of being free and released. The only difference was that I'd been hit hard and suddenly. What had happened to him gradually in weeks had happened to me in minutes. Maybe this was the only difference.

We could agree, too, that this release of ours was a gift, mysterious but real. He handed me [a] book. He hadn't read much of it but said that some of his Oxford Group friends thought it a fine explanation of religious conversion.

The moment Ebby left, I picked up the book and commenced to read. The title was *The Varieties of Religious Experience*. The author [was] William James, called by some the father of modern psychology. The book was not easy reading, but I kept at it all day. By nightfall, this Harvard professor, long in his grave, had, without anyone knowing it, become a founder of Alcoholics Anonymous. Dr. Jung, Dr. Silkworth, and the Oxford Groupers had already set candles upon the table around which our society was to arrange itself. William James had lighted still another.

The book consisted of careful accounts of very large numbers of religious or conversion experiences, and underneath each the professor had written a studious analysis. Here was another man who didn't think these experiences were hallucinations. His was the keenest sort of insight, accompanied by a most sympathetic understanding.

William James was an intellectual and, as I have said, the book was tough reading, but after a time I began to see that all the experiences cited, or at least nearly all of them, had certain common denominators, despite the variety of ways in which they manifested themselves.

The first common denominator was calamity. Nearly every recipient described had met utter defeat in some controlling area of his life. Every resource of courage, understanding, and will had failed. Each had beat in despair upon a wall and had seen no way over, under, or around. This was an essential condition of the experience to follow.

The next condition was the admission from the very depths of being that defeat was utter and absolute. Each individual had to concede that he simply couldn't go on living upon his own steam.

The third condition was an appeal to a higher power for help. This appeal could take innumerable forms. It might be accompanied by a faith in God or it might not, but an appeal it had to be. The cry for help could course through religious channels, or a despairing agnostic could look at a growing tree and, reflecting how the tree could respond to the law of its own nature and he, the human, could not, he might raise his voice to the god of nature.

Then the transforming experience would set in—sometimes like a thundercloud, as with St. Paul on the road to Damascus; or very gradually, following repeated appeals, the individual would slowly grow into a new state of consciousness and release.

Utter defeat, the completed mission of helplessness, and the appeal. These were the essential things.[12]

Within this simple frame of reference it was easy to pinpoint my own case. The god of science, my god in the person of a benign little doctor, had pronounced me hopeless, and I had accepted the verdict. I had made my appeal, and the result was forthcoming. But that wasn't all. Countless alcoholics before me had known of their hopelessness and had learned of it from medical men, yet they had received no gifts. They just deteriorated, went mad, and finally died. The difference between these cases and my own was not hard to see.

---

12. Editor's note—Here, Bill stops to change the tape. He then begins where he had left off: "Side 2, record 8, Hotel Bedford, September 1954. On side 1 I have described my spiritual experience, and am now in the process of analyzing. Here we go."

The difference lay in my relation to my friend Ebby, himself a onetime hopeless alcoholic. As a fellow sufferer he could, and did, identify himself with me as no other person could. As a recent dweller in the strange world of alcoholism he could, in memory, reenter it and stand by me in the cave where I was. Everybody else had to stand on the outside looking in. But he could enter, take me by the hand, and confidently lead me out.

On his first approach he was the bearer of bad news, but also of good news. The bad news was that I couldn't recover on my own resources, and that was a bitter, humiliating dose. But he had proved it out of his own experience, and out of the experience of alcoholics everywhere. He clinched this point, too, by telling me what Dr. Jung, the man of science, had said to Rowland.

The difference lay in my relation to my friend Ebby, himself a onetime hopeless alcoholic.

While Dr. Silkworth had deeply shaken my confidence in my own ability to recover, Ebby had somehow completely shattered it. His transmission line could reach into me at great depth. When he telegraphed the news of hopelessness over the cable of common understanding and common suffering, I had collapsed completely and at depth. One alcoholic had been talking to another as none other could. He had made me ready for the gift of release. He had then held his own gift up for me to see. He was the living proof of all he claimed. Nothing theoretical or secondhand about this.

When my rebellion was done, I saw, I believed, and I followed it. That had been the missing link: one alcoholic talking to another, bearing hopelessness in one hand and hope in the other. I could make my own choice, and that I had done.

As these realizations burst in upon me I became wildly excited. It was not daylight-clear why the clergymen's advice "You can do it, but only with God's help" hadn't worked. By contrast, Rowland, Ebby, and I had admitted that we of ourselves couldn't do anything at all. Nearly all the cases cited by Professor James had made the same admission. They, of themselves, couldn't do a thing about their several dilemmas. Before they could receive the gift, their self-confidence had to be destroyed—absolutely destroyed. Ego deflation at great depth was the key to the riddle. The sociologists and psychologists who would restore self-confidence had been mistaken. God-confidence was the thing, not self-confidence.

But how were alcoholics, agnostics, atheists, and those of faith long ago destroyed—how were such people to find confidence in a God they thought nonexistent? That had always been a poser. But now the answer seemed clear: Provided their personal hopelessness was great enough, an appeal to any higher power at all would bring results. They only needed to cry out in the dark for whomever or whatever might be there. No faith would be required. That would be part of the gift itself. Of this I was now perfectly sure, for this had been exactly the case with both Ebby and me. We had both humbly, and indeed hopelessly, asked, and the faith had come.

The moment the admission of hopelessness ran deep enough, any alcoholic could begin to receive faith and release. And one alcoholic turning the message to another could ready the sufferer for his gift as nobody else could.

At this point my excitement became boundless. A chain reaction could be set in motion, forming an evergrowing fellowship of alcoholics, whose mission it would be to visit the caves of still other sufferers and set them free. As each dedicated himself to carrying the message to still another, and those released to still others, such a society could pyramid to tremendous proportions. Why, it could reach every single alcoholic in the world capable of being honest enough to admit his own defeat. There must be millions of them, the alcoholics who still didn't know.

The Oxford Groups were then on the crest of public success and notice. Lois and I began attending meetings at Calvary

House, adjacent to Calvary Episcopal Church on Fourth Avenue in New York.

Here we first met Sam Shoemaker, dynamic rector of the church and one of the founders of the OG. In the hall of Calvary House and sometimes in the church, we listened to Sam and to the group's other leaders. These and the stories of Oxford Groupers we soon met made a lasting mark upon our lives. Never had we seen life so promising; never had an experience been richer.

On the platform and off, men and women, old and young, told how their lives had been transformed by the confession of their sins and restitution for harms done, dependence upon God for His guidance in all things. Travelers came from abroad reporting how God had claimed one country after another.

Travelers came from abroad reporting how God had claimed one country after another.

British nobility and world statesmen of note testified. So did union bosses and hod carriers; so did yellow people and colored people. Big business was there; so were clerks, salesmen, and typists. Rich and poor, socialites and commoners mingled happily in the common cause, in the great cause. Social, political, religious, and racial lines seemed almost nonexistent. Little was heard of theology, but we heard plenty of Absolute Honesty, Absolute Purity, Absolute Unselfishness, and Absolute Love. Confession, restitution, and direct guidance of God underlined every conversation. They were talking about morality and spirituality, about God-centeredness versus self-centeredness; they were talking about personal conversion and the conversion of the whole world. Everybody, good and bad, needed changing, they said.

Lois and I could certainly understand this. To have found a group of people so dedicated, so sincere, so confident, so eager, and so alive—well, in Lois and me this was manna from heaven. It was the difference between bright noonday and midnight as the spirit of these folks possessed us. Our enthusiasm knew no bounds. Heaven was our destination, and the world our oyster. We plunged headlong into the feverish activity about us. The life-giving water was wonderful, and we splashed joyously for some time.

At first sight the Oxford Group seemed to be one-time good people who had now become incomparably better. But we presently discovered that the cause had its problem children like we were. There were broken marriages, unhappy homes, and affairs of the heart gone wrong. Fortunes had been lost and never remade. Some had experienced crushing business and social defeat. Others had been wandering about, afraid, insecure, and alone. Others had drunk deep of bitterness and envy, having no purpose but retaliation. Some had been materially comfortable, yet bored still with life.

Then we found a sprinkling who had sins on the unmentionable side—a queer or so, and a jailbird. But most interesting of all were the alcoholics. One had headed a large advertising firm, but while interviewing an industrial tycoon had fallen flat on his face in broad daylight. This and extreme delirium tremens had brought him to the Oxford Group, where he was one of their most ardent workers, sober for some years.

At Calvary's mission there was Tex Francisco and Billy Duval, terrible cases, but happily sober a long time. And of course there were Rowland and Cebra and Shep, the three who straightened out my friend Ebby.

At the mission, a somewhat remote subsidiary fringing on the Oxford Group, we could of course find alcoholics in all states, mostly persistent disrepair. I . . . spotted these [alcoholics] at once as the possible nucleus of my dreamed-of project for sobering all the drunks in the world. Here was raw material aplenty.

. . . it soon appeared the Oxford Groupers weren't too much interested in drunks as such.

But it soon appeared the Oxford Groupers weren't too much interested in drunks as such. With very few exceptions the alcoholics had given them a bad time. Just before Lois and I appeared, the groupers had lodged several alcoholics in the upstairs bedrooms of Calvary House, the more respectable type of alcoholic coming from the well-to-do family. These hadn't done any better or as well as the boys at the mission. When one in a moment of alcoholic petulance had cast his shoe out of his bedroom, across the alley, and into a fine stained-glass window of Calvary Church, the Oxford Group figured that they'd better stick to their mission of changing the world and leave the drunks until later. Not that any who aspired to salvation should be denied. It was simply felt that more prudence and discrimination would be in order.

Not knowing this at first, I began to spend long hours at the mission. Many of the mission boys, when sober enough, would attend Oxford Group meetings, and then we'd all go to its Stewart's Cafeteria, talking on into the night.

Good old Dr. Silkworth, at the risk of his reputation, let me talk to some of his patients at Towns Hospital. Burning with confidence and enthusiasm, I pursued alcoholics morning, noon, and night. Though I made a few feeble efforts to get a job, these were soon forgotten in the excitement of the chase. Lois went on working at her department store, content with my new mission in the world.

Soon I was asked to speak at an Oxford Group meeting in Calvary House. The hall was packed, and so was the balcony. I told what I knew about alcoholism and all about my wonderful spiritual experience. Before finishing I saw a man in the second row. He had a very red face. All attention, he never took his eyes off me.

The moment the meeting was done he rushed up and, grabbing me by my lapels, told me how he was an alcoholic too; how I was the first man he'd ever talked to who knew the pitch. He was a professor of chemistry, barely holding his position. He said that his wife was in Oxford Group, but that he hadn't been able to go along. As a scientist and atheist, he couldn't simply stand all the nonsensical talk about God, nor did he like all these aggressive people who were trying to save his soul. His wife had dragged him to the meeting, and he had gone to keep peace in the family. While, of course, he couldn't go along with that weird religious experience of mine, he certainly did agree with what I said about alcoholism. He didn't need any religion, though he conceded that my own illusion might be doing me some good. What he needed, he said, was fellowship and more knowledge of alcoholism.

When I suggested the group of alcoholics to him, within the Oxford Group, of course, he really took fire, and soon became a nightly visitant at the mission and at Stewart's Cafeteria.

I was overjoyed. It looked like he was a surefire convert. If talking from a platform would produce results like this, I ought to do more of it, I thought. I decided on the spot that I liked public speaking. I could hardly imagine that my first new convert was to stay drunk eleven years thereafter.

The rest of the audience that night was attentive, but hardly enthusiastic. At the time I didn't notice this, let alone see the reason.

Afterword

This afterword gives an overview of Bill Wilson's remaining thirty-six years, the years after the taped recollection ends. He is sober after his treatment at Towns Hospital and his attendance at Oxford Group meetings. Bill began to gather with other Oxford Group members after meetings led by Rev. Dr. Samuel Shoemaker. He sought out alcoholics at Towns Hospital and Calvary Mission, trying to carry the message of hope that had helped him. After six months, the only one sober was Bill.

Bill tried to pick up his job prospects on Wall Street and was finally given an assignment to investigate a company in Akron, Ohio. Staying at the Mayflower Hotel, with the mounting tension of possibly drinking again and the assignment not working out, Bill reached out for help. As the story goes, Bill began calling churches from the lobby sign. Henrietta Seiberling finally assisted him, arranging a meeting with an active alcoholic. At Henrietta's home the next day he met Robert Holbrook Smith, M.D. Dr. Bob, as he is referred to around the world, was an alcoholic who had attempted to stay sober by attending Oxford Group meetings in Akron.

During the next month, Bill visited with Dr. Bob

frequently, emphasizing the alcoholism ideas from Dr. William Silkworth, the conversion ideas from William James, and the spiritual principles from the Oxford Group. On June 10, 1935, Dr. Bob took his last drink. This date is commemorated every year as the birthday of Alcoholics Anonymous, cofounded by Bill and Bob. The fledgling society would not use the name Alcoholics Anonymous (AA) until 1938.

Bill was invited to stay at the Smith home on Ardmore and use the bedroom of Sue, Anne and Bob's daughter. Many view the next three months, in the summer of 1935, as the most crucial for the beginnings of AA. Bill's letter to Lois, in appendix C, gives a powerful glimpse of this period. Anne Smith was an important influence on the newly sober Bill and Bob. Her years of attending Oxford Group meetings had made her the spiritual teacher both men desperately needed on a daily basis.[1]

Bill and Bob visited a notorious drunk, Bill Dotson, who was once again in the hospital. "AA Number Three" listened to their message and stayed sober. The miracle displayed through active fellowship had begun. At the end of the summer, a few more stayed sober as Bill returned to New York. Over the next two years, a few dozen drunks got sober in New York and Akron while attending Oxford Group

---

1. Charlotte Hunter, Billye Jones, and Joan Zieger, *Women Pioneers in Twelve Step Recovery* (Center City, Minn.: Hazelden, 1999), 1-23.

meetings as their "home group." The sober men began to refer to themselves as the "Alcoholic Squad" of the Oxford Group. Scores of alcoholics found recovery in the Oxford Group who were not associated with Bill or Bob.[2]

The growth of numbers was far more spectacular in Cleveland, under the leadership of Clarence Snyder who got sober with the help of Bob. Some may argue, but the tradition of "sponsorship" and the name Alcoholics Anonymous originated in Cleveland.[3] By 1938 the Alcoholic Squad was restless and fed up with the Oxford Group's emphasis on celebrities, wealthy individuals, and political leaders. These dissatisfactions prompted Bill to capture in writing how the earliest members of what would become AA had achieved and sustained their sobriety.

Bill and Bob decided to put together, in book form, their shared experience of the previous three years. Hank Parkhurst, a sober member of Bill's Squad in New York, wrote an outline for Bill to follow while writing the chapters of the book. Bob and the Cleveland Squads were assigned to put together the personal stories. Financing of the project was accomplished by selling stock certificates.

2. Dick B., *The Akron Genesis of Alcoholics Anonymous* (Kihei, Hawaii: Paradise Research Publications, Inc., 1998). Dick B. has written more than ten other books relating to the history of the Oxford Group and the beginnings of AA in Akron.
3. Mitchell K., *How It Worked: The Story of Clarence H. Snyder* (New York: AA Big Book Study Group, 1997). A full account of early AA in Cleveland.

The prospectus and basic ideas of the Squads' teachings are included in appendix D. Charles Towns, head of an alcoholism treatment hospital, was the biggest financial backer of the book project.

Bill wrote in longhand and had his secretary, Ruth Hock, type his writings and send them to Akron for review. A sample of the way Bill drafted his ideas is displayed in appendix B. Bill, in the years that followed, considered his writing of the first 164 pages of the AA text as "the umpire" of the project. Heated debates occurred over which ideas of the Oxford Group to include in the text. Taking the ideas of Dr. Silkworth for Step One and expanding on Oxford Group principles for the remaining Steps, the writing groups agreed on the important foundation of their program.[4]

The book *Alcoholics Anonymous*, commonly called the Big Book, was published in the spring of 1939. For the next two years, Bill was disappointed in the slow sales of the book. A positive article about the new fellowship appeared in the *Saturday Evening Post* on March 1, 1941. Bill and Ruth Hock were the two workers at the office of AA when 6,000 inquiries poured in following the article. The 1940s was a time of trial and error for AA as its membership grew in the United States and Canada. Many AA groups reported high

---

4. Visit the Hazelden-Pittman Museum of Addiction and Recovery at www.h-pmuseum.org for a full account of the writing of the Big Book.

recovery success rates.[5] Bill began to formulate and publish his ideas, which would guide and protect AA in 1946, calling them the Twelve Traditions. At the First International Convention of AA in 1950 these Traditions were adopted. The Traditions have been vital guidelines for AA as an organization and have protected AA from the kinds of controversy that have ended many other movements.

On November 16, 1950, Bob died from cancer. Although his involvement spanned only fifteen years, his many influences are still present in AA today. A major part of the success of AA can be attributed to the great bond and friendship of the two cofounders. Bill's "big picture" ideas were grounded in Bob's commitment to keep AA simple. This unique mix of personalities offset any character defects. Bob is also remembered for his contribution to the field of alcoholism, having worked with Sister Mary Ignatia Gavin to establish an alcoholic unit at Saint Thomas Hospital in Akron.[6]

Bill's early years in AA reflected his incredible drive and effort to rein in his own grandiosity and desire for fame and glory—an effort in which he was greatly aided by Bob and by

---

5. Wally P., *Back to Basics: The Alcoholics Anonymous "Beginners' Classes"* (Tucson, Ariz.: Faith with Works Publishing Company, 1997). Overview of AA's "Beginner's Classes" in the 1940s.
6. Mary C. Darrah, *Sister Ignatia: Angel of Alcoholics Anonymous* (Chicago: Loyola University Press, 1992). Biography of Sister Ignatia and her work with alcoholics.

Father Ed Dowling, Bill's spiritual advisor.[7] Bill's refusal of an employment offer by Towns Hospital, in spite of his acute poverty, marked a milestone in both Bill's and AA's history. This decision is remarkable when one considers that, from 1939 to 1941, Bill and Lois were so poor that they lived out of suitcases with friends and AA members. And yet something in Bill's character and generosity is evident in his appeal for financial support from the Guggenheim Foundation during this period—not for himself, but for Bob and Anne.

While continuing his recovery and work within AA, Bill suffered from serious bouts of depression. In 1944 he began undergoing psychotherapy twice a week with Dr. Harry Tiebout.[8] Bill's battle with depression gave him a deep appreciation of the psychological problems that often accompany and are masked by alcoholism. Bill's bouts with depression were very hard to bear, particularly when some fellow AA members attributed Bill's depression to not working the Twelve Steps.

Bill was very interested in religion and even took Catholic instruction for a period, but he never joined any particular church. Bill, like the program he helped create, could be

7. Robert Fitzgerald, S.J., *The Soul of Sponsorship: The Friendship of Fr. Ed Dowling, S.J., and Bill Wilson in Letters* (Center City, Minn.: Hazelden, 1995). Insightful account of the friendship of these two men.
8. *Harry Tiebout: The Collected Writings* (Center City, Minn.: Hazelden, 1999). This volume brings together Tiebout's most influential writings about alcoholism and AA.

described as deeply spiritual but not religious. AA members often say, "Religion is for people who don't want to go to hell; AA is for those that have been there." Bill, far from being deified within AA, was the subject of ruthless and severe criticism, often unsubstantiated, from fellow AA members. He was most often criticized for his obsessions—the Twelve Traditions and AA self-government—and for not attending AA meetings on a consistent basis.

In accordance with AA's tradition of anonymity, Bill turned down many offers during his lifetime: an honorary doctoral degree in law from Yale University, a listing in *Who's Who in America,* and an opportunity to appear on the cover of *Time* magazine. In spite of the personal recognition that came to him and to AA, he continued during the last fifteen years of his life to explore new approaches that might help people who struggle with, or fail to understand and accept, the AA program. While the overall AA program moved toward stability and maturity, Bill still seemed obsessed with those who somehow weren't able to make AA work for them. Warning of the dangers of pride and complacency, he challenged AA members at AA's thirtieth anniversary meeting with a question: "What happened to the 600,000 who approached AA and left?"

From his home in Bedford Hills, New York, Bill explored subjects outside of his official position in AA. He studied vitamin B-3 and LSD in an attempt to explain why many couldn't stay sober. Bill became interested in these areas through his encounter with two psychiatrists, Dr. Humphry Osmond and Dr. Abram Hoffer, who were pioneering the use of vitamin B-3 and LSD in the treatment of alcoholism.

In addition to the Big Book, Bill Wilson had other royalty contracts with AA headquarters: *Twelve Steps and Twelve Traditions* (1952), *Alcoholics Anonymous Comes of Age* (1957) and *As Bill Sees It* (1967). Bill also authored *The AA Service Manual and Twelve Concepts for World Service* (1962). The *Service Manual* outlines all the activities of AA groups, AA's board of trustees, the general service office, and the magazine of the fellowship, the *AA Grapevine*. The annual meeting of delegates and the trustees from the United States and Canada may vote to change the *Service Manual*. Although Bill turned over the fellowship to the General Service Conference of AA in 1955, along with his ideas in the *Service Manual* and other writings, Bill still has a significant influence on AA today.

As we enter the twenty-first century, many great history books have been written about the life of Bill Wilson and the fellowship of AA. Many more history books will follow. In his award-winning book, *Slaying the Dragon: The History of Addiction Treatment and Recovery in America*, William White sums up Bill Wilson's life in this way:

When Bill turned the fellowship over to the General Service Board, he noted that A.A. was now safe even from him. This point is a crucial one. What is most striking to this author about the life of Bill Wilson is his admirable struggle to set aside personal ambition for the broader good of A.A. His refusal of employment at the Towns Hospital, correction of his early breaches of anonymity, his admonishment that A.A. leaders had to be "on tap, not on top," and the ability to resist his need for control and allow A.A. to mature beyond its founders are all testaments to his success in this struggle. What is even more remarkable is how conscious his efforts were: Bill talked often about how his efforts to dampen his insatiable pursuit of money, fame, and power with alcohol had almost killed him, but he also talked about his awareness that the dreaded "neurotic germ of the power contagion" had survived inside him.[9]

In 1947 a young women, Nell Wing, came to work at AA headquarters. From 1950 until his death, Nell was Bill's administrative assistant. Nell said of Bill: "He devoted a large part of his energy and time to trying to divest himself of power and authority, instead of trying to hang onto them."[10]

---

9. William L. White, *Slaying the Dragon: The History of Addiction Treatment and Recovery in America* (Bloomington, Ill.: Chestnut Health Systems/Lighthouse Institute, 1998), 139. The above brief sketch of Bill Wilson is drawn from William White's material with his cooperation.

10. Nell Wing, *Grateful to Have Been There: My Forty-two Years with Bill and Lois, and the Evolution of Alcoholics Anonymous*, 2d ed. (Center City, Minn.: Hazelden, 1998). Nell recounts her forty-two-year relationship with Bill and Lois Wilson and the evolution of AA.

With the help of people like Father Dowling, Dr. Tiebout, Earl Marsh, Bob, Nell, Lois, and others, and through his daily struggle to master the very program he helped found, Bill achieved enough detachment to allow AA to grow into its own.

There will be future historical revelations about Bill's character and behavior in recovery that will be interpreted, by some, as direct attacks on the very foundation of AA. Bill often wished he could be just another AA member with no trace of notoriety. But such revelations will, in the end, only reinforce Bill's humanness and, most important, the extent to which Bill acted to the best of his ability to protect AA from himself. We are reminded of one of AA's adopted slogans, "But for the grace of God, go I."

Bill Wilson died on his and Lois's fifty-third wedding anniversary, January 24, 1971. As he was a heavy smoker all his life, emphysema was the cause of death. Lois lived another seventeen years at the home she and Bill had named Stepping Stones. Bill's royalties, under the guidance of Lois, established the Stepping Stones Foundation, whose grants carry on work relating to alcoholism.

Bill wanted to write a last book called *After Sobriety, What?* He wanted to relate his experiences in recovery and what he had learned from others. He began the book by submitting chapters to the *AA Grapevine* for publication. Many agree that Bill's greatest statements about recovery and about his own recovery struggles are in his *AA Grapevine* article "The

Next Frontier: Emotional Sobriety." With over twenty years of sobriety, Bill wrote:

Those adolescent urges that so many of us have for top approval, perfect security, and perfect romance—urges quite appropriate to age seventeen—prove to be an impossible way of life when we are at age forty-seven or fifty-seven.[11]

Bill never completed the book, but we are grateful that the *AA Grapevine* has published a volume of Bill's writings entitled *The Language of the Heart.*

Bill Wilson was the first AA member to get sober within a facility that specialized in caring for alcoholics. The Twelve Steps, which he helped articulate, are used around the world today as a suggested program of recovery from alcoholism. AA is America's only therapeutic social movement dealing with alcoholics that didn't dwindle away after the deaths of its founders.

In 1984 Alcoholics Anonymous World Services published a biography of Bill entitled *Pass It On.* In the book's final pages is a description of Bill's obituary in *The New York Times,* the private memorial service at Stepping Stones, and the simple white marble gravestone in East Dorset Cemetery—the same marble his forefathers dug from the

---

11. *The Language of the Heart: Bill W.'s Grapevine Writings* (New York: The AA Grapevine, Inc., 1988), 236. A collection of over 100 of Bill W.'s *AA Grapevine* writings.

earth. On February 14, memorial services were held in churches around the world.

Bill's headstone humbly reads: William G. Wilson, 1895–1971. There is no mention of Alcoholics Anonymous.

Additional Recommended Reading

Alcoholics Anonymous Comes of Age: A Brief History of A.A.
New York: Alcoholics Anonymous World Services, Inc.,
1957.
*Dr. Bob and the Good Oldtimers: A Biography, with
Recollections of Early A.A. in the Midwest.* New York:
Alcoholics Anonymous World Services, Inc., 1980.
Kurtz, Ernest. *Not-God: A History of Alcoholics Anonymous.*
Center City, Minn.: Hazelden, 1991.
*Lois Remembers: Memoirs of the Co-founder of Al-Anon and
Wife of the Co-founder of Alcoholics Anonymous.* New York:
Al-Anon Family Group Headquarters, Inc., 1979.
Thomsen, Robert. *Bill W.* Center City, Minn.: Hazelden,
1999. This is the trade paperback edition, published by
arrangement with HarperCollins. The original edition,
which is currently out of print, was published by Harper
and Row in 1975.

APPENDIXES

Appendix A

THE HEALER
BILL W.

By Susan Cheever

Susan Cheever, a novelist and memoirist, is the author of
Note Found in a Bottle: My Life as a Drinker.

econd Lieut. Bill Wilson didn't think twice when
the first butler he had ever seen offered him a
drink. The 22-year-old soldier didn't think about
how alcohol had destroyed his family. He didn't
think about the Yankee temperance movement of
his childhood or his loving fiancé Lois Burnham
or his emerging talent for leadership. He didn't think about
anything at all. "I had found the elixir of life," he wrote.
Wilson's last drink, 17 years later, when alcohol had
destroyed his health and his career, precipitated an epiphany
that would change his life and the lives of millions of other
alcoholics. Incarcerated for the fourth time at Manhattan's
Towns Hospital in 1934, Wilson had a spiritual awaken-
ing—a flash of white light, a liberating awareness of God—
that led to the founding of Alcoholics Anonymous and
Wilson's revolutionary 12-step program, the successful rem-
edy for alcoholism. The 12 steps have also generated successful programs for eating disorders, gambling, narcotics,

debting, sex addiction and people affected by others' addictions. Aldous Huxley called him "the greatest social architect of our century."

William Griffith Wilson grew up in a quarry town in Vermont. When he was 10, his hard-drinking father headed for Canada, and his mother moved to Boston, leaving the sickly child with her parents. As a soldier, and then as a businessman, Wilson drank to alleviate his depressions and to celebrate his Wall Street success. Married in 1918, he and Lois toured the country on a motorcycle and appeared to be a prosperous, promising young couple. By 1933, however, they were living on charity in her parents' house on Clinton Street in Brooklyn, N.Y. Wilson had become an unemployable drunk who disdained religion and even panhandled for cash.

Inspired by a friend who had stopped drinking, Wilson went to meetings of the Oxford Group, an evangelical society founded in Britain by Pennsylvania Frank Buchman. And as Wilson underwent a barbiturate-and-belladonna cure called "purge and puke," which was state-of-the-art alcoholism treatment at the time, his brain spun with phrases from Oxford Group meetings, Carl Jung and William James' Varieties of Religious Experience, which he read in the hospital. Five sober months later, Wilson went to Akron, Ohio, on business. The deal fell through, and he wanted a drink. He stood in the lobby of the Mayflower Hotel, entranced by the sounds of the bar across the hall.

Appendix A

Suddenly he became convinced that by helping another alcoholic, he could save himself.

Through a series of desperate telephone calls, he found Dr. Robert Smith, a skeptical drunk whose family persuaded him to give Wilson 15 minutes. Their meeting lasted for hours. A month later, Dr. Bob had his last drink, and that date, June 10, 1935, is the official birth date of A.A., which is based on the idea that only an alcoholic can help another alcoholic. "Because of our kinship in suffering," Bill wrote, "our channels of contact have always been charged with the language of the heart."

The Burnham house on Clinton Street became a haven for drunks. "My name is Bill W., and I'm an alcoholic," he told assorted houseguests and visitors at meetings. To spread the word, he began writing down his principles for sobriety. Each chapter was read by the Clinton Street group and sent to Smith in Akron for more editing. The book had a dozen provisional titles, among them *The Way Out* and *The Empty Glass*. Edited to 400 pages, it was finally called *Alcoholics Anonymous*, and this became the group's name.

But the book, although well reviewed, wasn't selling. Wilson tried unsuccessfully to make a living as a wire-rope salesman. A.A. had about a hundred members, but many were still drinking. Meanwhile, in 1939, the bank foreclosed on the Clinton Street house, and the couple began years of homelessness, living as guests in borrowed rooms and at one point staying in temporary quarters above the A.A. clubhouse on 24th Street in Manhattan. In 1940 John D. Rockefeller Jr. held an A.A. dinner and was impressed enough to create a trust to provide Wilson with $30 a week—but no more. The tycoon felt that money would corrupt the group's spirit.

Then, in March 1941, the *Saturday Evening Post* published an article on A.A., and suddenly thousand of letters and requests poured in. Attendance at meetings doubled and tripled. Wilson had reached his audience. In *Twelve Traditions*, Wilson set down the suggested bylaws of Alcoholics Anonymous. In them, he created an enduring blueprint for an organization with a maximum of individual freedom and no accumulation of power or money. Public anonymity ensured humility. No contributions were required; no member could contribute more than $1,000.

Today more than 2 million A.A. members in 150 countries hold meetings in church basements, hospital conference rooms and school gyms, following Wilson's informal structure. Members identify themselves as alcoholics and share their stories; there are no rules or entry requirements, and many members use only first names.

Wilson believed the key to sobriety was a change of heart. The suggested 12 steps include an admission of powerlessness, a moral inventory, a restitution for harm done, a call to service and a surrender to some personal God. In A.A., God can be anything from a radiator to a patriarch. Influenced by A.A., the American Medical Association has redefined alcoholism as a chronic disease, not a failure of willpower.

As Alcoholics Anonymous grew, Wilson became its principal symbol. He helped create a governing structure for the program, the General Service Board, and turned over his power. "I have become a pupil of the A.A. movement rather than the teacher," he wrote. A smoker into his 70s, he died of pneumonia and emphysema in Miami, where he went for treatment in 1971. To the end, he clung to the principles and the power of anonymity. He was always Bill W., refusing to take money for counseling and leadership. He turned down many honors, including a degree from Yale. And he declined this magazine's offer to put him on the cover—even with his back turned.

BORN Nov. 26, 1895, in East Dorset, Vt.

1918 Marries Lois Burnham. In 1951 she founds Al-Anon for families of alcoholics

1933 First of four hospitalizations for alcoholism

1934 Takes his last drink

1935 Persuades Dr. Robert Smith to stay sober with him. This is the first A.A. meeting

1938 Forms the Alcoholics Foundation

1939 Publishes the book *Alcoholics Anonymous*, which includes the 12 steps

1953 Publishes *Twelve Steps and Twelve Traditions*, outlining a structure for A.A.

DIED Jan. 24, 1971, of pneumonia, in Miami

Appendix B

The Strange Obsession

It was last night
in its midsummer of 1934.
I found myself at a noted
address on Central Park West,
New York City. It was at the Charlie
Towns hospital for drying out
alcoholics.

Shaking and sweltering
out a fearful hangover
I was taken in an
upstairs room. Sometimes
the doctor looked across
his desk at my wife Lois.

She was saying "Doctor,
why can't he
stop drinking? He always had
good will power. Yet here he
is, facing me again,
and still he can't
stop. The more he struggles
the worse he gets. I am confused.
I know he wants to. He'd do
anything — anything at
all to stop. Tell me, doctor,
why can't he?"

The Strange Obsession

It was a hot night in the midsummer of 1934. I found myself at a noted address in Central Park West New York City. It was in Charlie Towns hospital for drying out alcoholics.

Sobering and sweltering out a fearful hangover I laid abed in an upstairs room. Downstairs the doctor looked across his desk at my wife Lois.

She was saying, "Doctor, why can't Bill stop drinking? He always had great willpower. Yet here he is, facing ruin again, and still he can't stop. The more he struggles, the worse he gets. I am scared, heartbroken and confused. I know he is, too. He'd do anything—anything at all to stop. Tell me, Doctor, why can't he?"

Lois was asking the same
terrible question that uncounted
women had asked before.
It's was a riddle quite
as old as man first discovery
that alcohol could be made
from grapes and grains.

Again she said "Please
tell me the truth doctor. Why
can't Bill stop?"

In his long experience with
serious drinkers the good doctor had faced
that heartbreaker a thousand
times. By nature ~~both~~ ~~the~~
even passionate human
failed to wince whenever a
distraught wife husband or
friend who suffered propounded
anew the ancient riddle of
alcoholism. Bill Silkworth had
wondered and moved him
deeply. How could he now bring
himself to tell Lois the truth.

Appendix B

Lois was asking the same terrible question that uncounted women had asked before. Her's was a riddle quite as old as mans first discovery that alcohol could be made from grapes and grains.

Again she said, "Please tell me the truth doctor. Why can't Bill stop?"

In his long experience with serious drinkers the good doctor had faced that terrible heartbreaker a thousand times. By nature compassionate, he never failed to wince whenever a distraught wife husband or friend of a sufferer had profounded anew the burdened riddle of alcoholism. Bill's dilemma had interested and moved him deeply. How could he now bring himself to tell Lois the truth?

genial little doctor's

The face turned grave as
began to speak. "When Bill
first came to this hospital
three years ago, I felt that
he might be one of those
rare cases who **might recover**
~~a permanent~~. I
hoped that when he better
understood himself and
the nature of his illness,
he might **win out**.
In spite of a decided
severe relapses since then,
I have gone on hoping.
For, as you say, he
desperately wants to quit
and his will to do so is
very great. But now I've
about managed. I'm afraid
he's going to be like. Nearly
all the other alcoholics ~~that~~
~~who come~~ my way.

"Well Doctor" cried Lois "
just what do you mean
by that. Won't he ever
get better"

The benign little doctors face turned grave as [he] began to speak. "When Bill first came to this hospital three years ago, I felt that he might be one of those rare cases who might recover. I hoped that when he better understood himself and the nature of his illness, he might win out. In spite of his several severe relapses since then, I have gone on hoping. For, as you say, he desperately wants to quit and his will to do so is very great. But now I'm discouraged. I'm afraid he's going to be like nearly all the other alcoholics who come my way.

"Well Doctor" cried Lois "just what do you mean by that. Won't he ever get better?"

~~And so Gently,~~ the Doctor went on " As you already understood, your husband is a sick man. ~~though the~~ ~~there is here to tell you~~ more about his illness and how really serious his condition now is.

Gently, the Doctor went on " Mrs W— said, you already know that your husband is a sick man. But I've never told you just how sick an alcoholic can be, nor have I ever explained this illness to you as I understand it from my long observation. There are a lot of theories about the underlying causes of compulsive drinking like Bill's. Of these we can take our pick. But there are some solid facts, too, which no one who has watched ~~many~~ alcoholics could well dispute."

Appendix B

Gently, the Doctor went on "As you already understand, your husband is a sick man. I think the time is here to tell you more about his illness and how really serious his condition now is.

Gently, the Doctor went on "Mrs W. said he, you already know that your husband is a sick man. But I've never told you just how sick an alcoholic can be, nor have I ever explained this illness to you as I understand it from my long observation. There are a lot of theories about the underlying causes of complusive drinking like Bill's. Of these we can take our pick. But there are some solid facts, too, which no one who has watched many alcoholics could well dispute.

(5)

Fact one is that innumerable alcoholic men and women really want to ~~control their own~~ drinking and then find, to their dismay, that they cannot. They cannot moderate their drinking as other people do. Nor, even when faced with the most terrible consequences, can they stop altogether, no matter how desperate their plight. Never do the excuses they make for themselves ~~the~~ ~~making their~~ patterns of continuous self destruction. Their behavior becomes completely illogical and irrational—it really verges on insanity. And even when they well understand all this, they go on as before. Where alcohol is concerned, their minds no longer rule their emotions. ~~The~~

Fact one is that innumerable alcoholic men and women really want to control their destructive drinking and then find, to their dismay, that they cannot. They cannot moderate their drinking as other people do. Nor, even when faced with the most terrible consequences, can they stop altogether, no matter how desperate their plight. Never do the excuses they make for their sprees justify their pattern of continuous self destruction. Their behavior becomes completely illogical and irrational—it really verges on insanity. And even when they well understand all this, they go on as before. Where alcohol is concerned, their minds no longer rule their emotions.

6

A new spree can be
started upon the slightest
excuse — rationalizing.
Somehow the
provocations seem
seems great, but
always very small when
the seldom destructive
results are considered.
When life gives the average
man a heavy bump,
he doesn't rush to his
tool chest, take out
a hammer and beat
himself into insensibility.
Yet, in effect, that's what
the sick alcoholic does,
over and over. All reason,
all incentive, even
the greatest desire to stop,
seems to be swamped
when the craving for
alcohol takes hold.

The fact about alcoholism
is its obsessional nature.
It is one of the most subtle,
most powerful compulsions

Appendix B

A new spree can be started upon the [slightest of] excuses or rationalizations. Sometimes the provocations seems great, but its always very small when the certain destructive results are considered. When for example life gives the average man a heavy bump, he doesn't seize a hammer and beat himself into [insensibility]. Yet, in effect, that's what the sick alcoholic does, over and over. All reason, all incentive, even the greatest desire to stop, seems to be swamped when the craving for alcohol takes hold.

"Therefore the biggest fact about alcoholism is its obsessional nature. It is one of the most subtle yet most powerful compulsions

known. Once its grip is firm, the chance for recovery is slim indeed. How to help the alcoholic to expel his obsession is the problem. But we doctors have had little success; I've seldom helped even one case in a hundred"—

"Use is the drunkard's obsession, the whole story; alcoholism is physical malady too. In nearly all cases the bodies of problem drinkers become painfully sensitive to alcohol. But in the early stages some alcoholics can drink quantities of liquor without serious physical reactions. But continued excesses finally cause them to lose that ability"; they seem to get allergic to the stuff, so much so that hangovers produce great physical agony and sometimes delerium tremens or convulsions too often followed by brain damage and mental deterioration that

can be permanent.

known. Once it's grip is firm, the chance for recovery is diminished. How to help the alcoholic to expel his obsession is the problem. But we doctors have had little success: I've seldom helped even one case in a hundred."

"Nor is the drinkers obsession the whole story: alcoholism is a physical malady too. In nearly all cases the bodies of problem drinkers become painfully sensitive to alcohol. In the early stages of their malady some alcoholics can drink quantities of liquor without serious physical reaction. But continued excesses finally cause them to lose that ability; they seem to get allergic to the stuff; so much so that hangovers produce great physical agony and sometimes delirium tremens or convulsions too often followed by brain damage and mental deterioration that can be permanent.

Appendix C

W. G. W.
BOX 451
BEDFORD HILLS, N. Y. 10507

Dr. R. H. SMITH
Surgeon -928 Second Nat'l Bldg
Akron, Ohio

DARLING :
I am writing this in the office of one of my new
friends, Dr. Smith. He had my trouble and is getting to be
a very ardent Grouper. I have been to his house for meals
and the rest of the family is as nice as he is. I have
witnessed at a number of meetings and have been taken to a
number of people. Dr. Smith is helping me to change a
Dr. McKay, once the most prominent surgeon in town, who
developed into a terrific rake and drunk. He was rich,
lost everything, wife committed suicide, he is ostracised
and on the point of suicide himself. His change if accomplished, would be a most powerful witness to the whole
town as his case is so notorious.

I was infinitely relieved to get your note saying the insurance is paid. It seems very hard to burden
Howard with it. Make it clear to him about the bonus and
momey from the Boss. I certainly wish we had more slack
but it can't be helped.

I am sorry I was blue yesterday. There is supposed
to be an inspection tomorrow but I have my fingers crossed.

Am very anxious to hear what the Boss says. I
should have written him in the first instance, as Carrie
probably got her eye on that check.

We do make progress however – The lawyer, De
Ueigis has resigned from the board.

I love you so very much and know it is so hard
for you to wait there alone. Anyhow, for the first time
in my life – I know I am doing my best at a really worth-
while job.

Love, darling –
BILL

Appendix D

It occured [*sic*] to Mr. Wilson that accurate and reliable medical information should be in the possession of every alcoholic when he approached another alcoholic. With such equipment the new prospect could be readily persuaded that he was hopeless; that he is, in actual fact at the jumping off place.

Being convinced there was no other way out, the new man would look with more favor and willingness upon a spiritual method in spite of any prejudice he might have had.

In the spring of 1935 Mr. Wilson went to Akron, Ohio, on business. While there he communicated his ideas to three other alcoholics. Leaving the three men, he returned to New York in the fall of 1935, continuing his activities there. These early seeds are now bearing amazing fruit. The original Akron three have expanded themselves into more than seventy. Scattered about New York and in the seaboard states there are about forty. Men have even come out of insane asylums and resumed their community and family lives. Business and professional people have regained their standing.

In all, about two-hundred cases of hopeless alcoholism have been dealt with. As will be seen, about fifty percent of these have recovered. This, of course, is unprecedented—never has such a thing happened before.

This work has claimed the attention of prominent doctors and institutions who say without hesitation that in a few years time, as it gains impetous [*sic*], thousands of hitherto incurable cases may recover. Such people as the chief physician of Charles B. Towns Hospital and psychiatrists of the Johns Hopkins Hospital at Baltimore express such opinions.

THE PRESENT PROGRAM

It has been felt vitally necessary to spread the work widely and get it on a sound basis rapidly.

The first step has been the establishment of a trust known as The Alcoholic Foundation. This trust is administered by a board of three well-known business men who are non-alcoholics, and by two members of Alcoholics Anonymous. The articles of the trust specifically set forth that non-alcoholic members shall always be in a majority of one over the alcoholic members. The Alcoholic Foundation will, in order to obviate any possible criticism, administer the financial affairs of the group.

When it is considered that there are an estimated million alcoholics in this country the obligation for wide spread of the work may be perceived. Education and instruction should be made available to every one touched by a drink situation. An understanding of the nature of the disease and its cure must be mastered by wives, relatives and employers of alcoholics. A definite program of attitude and action should be offered everyone concerned. It is felt that these aims may be gained by the publishing of an anonymous volume based upon the past four years experience.

The publishing of this book, to be known as "One Hundred Men," is the subject of the attached material. The Alcoholic Foundation will receive an author's royalty as a donation for the furtherance of the work.

Considering the necessity for a volume of this kind; its being based upon actual experience; the publicity that has been assured; and the tremendous amount of good inherent in its result; anyone must agree with a former editor of the New York Times, who after reading the first two chapters predicted a sensational sale. (Ten chapters have now been written).

THE PROPOSAL
It is proposed to form—
"THE ONE HUNDRED MEN CORPORATION."

PURPOSE
To publish the book—"One Hundred Men."

ASSETS
Money has been subscribed to maintain the author for five months. A completely equipped office.

THE ISSUE
Sufficient $25.00 par value shares to promote publicity, sales, and publish the book. Shares either payable in full at time of subscription, or five dollars for each share subscribed at time of subscription and five dollars per share each thirty days for four months after subscription.

THE CORPORATION
Stock—Non-Assessable.   Delaware Corporation.

FACTS
The following facts are pertinent in considering the possible success of the volume—"One Hundred Men."

1. Publicity
2. Established Publisher's Opinion
3. The Possible Market.

PUBLICITY—1. Of publicity value is the fact that the foundational soundness of the work is verified by letters from The Johns Hopkins Hospital, and the chief physician of Charles B. Towns Hospital, one of the foremost alcoholic institutions in the United States. Furthermore the work has been investigated and justified most thoroughly by private parties from an outside source.

2. The syndicated magazine This Week, (included with Sunday

New York Herald Tribune and many other Sunday newspapers) has expressed an interest in running a page two article regarding the work and the forthcoming book. The editor prophesied from fifteen to twenty thousand inquiries from the weekly circulation of five million two hundred and fifty thousand. This syndicated magazine section for Sunday newspapers is second only to the American Weekly used by Hearst papers.

3. The Readers Digest, in a personal interview with the Managing Editor, stated that the work and the forthcoming volume were of such interest as to justify their placing a staff writer on it and running an exclusive article just prior to publication of the volume.

4. Mr. Wainright Evans, established author, wrote Mr. Bigelow, Editor of Good Housekeeping magazine, a letter regarding the work. Two of the members of Alcoholics Anonymous in company with Mr. Evans called upon Mr. Bigelow who requested Mr. Evans to submit an outline of the completed article which he believed would be used by the magazine just prior to the issuance of the book.

5. A fact pertinent to one's calculations as to the possible public interest should be the results of the publication last spring of an article entitled "The Unhappy Drinker" in the Saturday Evening Post. The Post commented that more inquiries came to them from this than from any other article they had ever printed.

6. Approximately a year ago a very obscure article was published by Doctor Silkworth in a small New York Medical journal. He barely alluded to this work, simply saying that such a thing was happening. He was amazed by the hundreds of inquiries received from lay people all over the United States.

7. Established publishers have said both directly and by implication that this volume seems assured of the most unusual publicity preceding publication of any book they have known.

ESTABLISHED PUBLISHERS OPINION—Established publishers must practically see a sure fire book in order to make an advance to an author. Furthermore they are exceptionally careful that this advance is conservative in order that it may be returned from royalties on sales. Harper & Bros. after reading the first two chapters, investigating the publicity, and talking to two members of Alcoholics Anonymous, offered fifteen hundred dollars as an advance against royalties. This is impressive in view of the fact that five thousand volumes would need to be sold to repay the advance.

In the course of publishing investigation, these same two members of Alcoholics Anonymous called upon Mr. Walsh, owner of the John Day Publishing Company, publishers of such volumes as The Good Earth, The Importance of Living, etc. This call was made upon the basis of a personal friendship with Mr. Walsh and as a consequence the advice given by him was upon a friendly basis rather than securing the publishing of the book. Not only did Mr. Walsh give invaluable printing, credit, and sales information, but predicted an unusual sale for the volume. He said, and gave reasons for his opinion which will be outlined later, that he could not see where this venture would gain through using an established publisher.

THE POSSIBLE MARKET—It has been estimated that there are over a million alcoholics in the United States and that every family seems touched by the problem. If this is so, and we have been assured that there has never been any published work that not only gave the answer, but told a man what to do to recover, then this book should have an incredible sale.

One Hundred Men will not only have an appeal to the alcoholic layman, and those affected, but should appeal to the five hundred thousand Clergymen in this country, the three hundred and fifty thousand Physicians, and the twenty odd thousand established Psychiatrists. We know that the problem is one of pressing concern to large corporations, and we know also that special reprints should be interesting to insurance companies.

Taken these few fundamental market facts into consideration, along with the publicity that seems assured, who can estimate the possible sale?

CORPORATE SET-UP

The corporation is set up on a budget that runs to April 1st. By that time the book will be out and further sales plans will need to be made upon experiences to date.

However for full protection of the shareholders the shareholders procedure will be set up in the articles of the corporation.

On each of the first 1000 books, eighty cents will be apportioned among the shareholders who have made a cash subscription.

On each of the second 1000 books, seventy cents will be apportioned among the shareholders.

On each book over 2000 books and until the subscriptions have been returned, sixty cents will be apportioned to the shareholders.

The difference between the above payments and the gross profit will accrue in the corporate treasury. It is planned to call a stockholders' meeting in March, 1939, to vote as to whether the corporation shall distribute cash on hand to the stockholders, or continue maintaining headquarters for the direct sales of the book.

BUDGET TO APRIL 1st, 1939.

Author. $1,000.000
Directional and Sales Promotional Work 1,800.00
Office Rent 480.00
Stenographer 650.00
Office Expense (estimated). 240.00
Incidental Expenses 500.00
Printing Plates 700.00
1000 Volumes. 350.00
Art Work 250.00
$5,970.00

Of the above, there has been extended as a loan to insure the writing of the volume $1,500.00

COSTS
Printing (highest figure assumed by Mr. Walsh)

per volume . . . . $.34
Royalty (to Alcoholic Foundation) 35
Packaging, drayage, etc. per volume 05
                                                         .74

SALES FIGURES
Retail price $3.00
Jobbers discount (maximum 46%) 1.38
                                                         1.62
Printing, royalty, and packaging 74
Gross profit per volume sold through bookstores. 88

Mr. Walsh estimated that as a result of the publicity, one volume at least would be sold for every two volumes through book stores. For direct sales the following costs would prevail.

Printing . . . .$.34
Royalty (to Alcoholic Foundation) 35
Packaging, drayage, addressing 12
Postage (highest) 12
                                                         .93
Gross profit one direct sale $2.07

Taking the estimate of one direct sale for two book store sales, we have the following set up:

Gross profit two book store sales @ 88 cents $1.76
Gross profit per volume one direct sale. $2.07
                                                         $3.83

Dividing by three we have an average gross profit of $1.276 per volume.

PROFITS

As said before any accurate estimating of profits cannot even be approached.

For anyone who wishes to draw their own estimate, the following figures and facts are given:

It would take sales of the first 5000 volumes (basis Harpers advance offer) by April first to assure subscribers money. Inasmuch as the budget has been designed to defray all expenses of operation to April 1st, profits up to that date are gross profits, without deductions.

On the other hand if office were maintained through April, May and June and five thousand volumes only were sold, the returns to the shareholders would be slightly over fifty percent. As mentioned before, decision as to continuance of the office through April, May and June, will be made at the stockholders' meeting in March, 1939.

If, on the other hand, any success such as has been predicted accrues, the following profit projection would seem possible.

By June first the subscription would have been returned. Then, if the following sales are reached the profit per share would be:

```
15,000 volumes first year—per share return after money back. . . . . . $10.00
25,000 . . . . . . . . . . . . . . . . . . . . .. . . . . . . . . . . . . . . . . . . . . . . . . . . . .. . . . . . . . . . . . . . 30.00
50,000 . . . . . . . . . . . . . . . . . . . . .. . . . . . . . . . . . . . . . . . . . . . . . . . . . .. . . . . . . . . . . . . . 75.00
100,000 . . . . . . . . . . . . . . . . . . . . .. . . . . . . . . . . . . . . . . . . . . . . . . . . . .. . . . . . . . . . . . 150.00
```

Although it seems ridiculous, one estimate has been made of half a million volumes within two years time. Should this come, over nine hundred dollars per share would be returned.

OPERATION OF THE
ONE HUNDRED MEN CORPORATION

During the time of the writing of the book, and while sales promotional and directional duties are going on, the necessity of an office is apparent.

Among other sales promotional possibilities that must be followed up is the offer of Floyd Parsons to write an article based upon the book for the Saturday Evening Post. Mr. Parsons is very well acquainted with the editor and believes an article would be acceptable.

Most of the church organizations have their National Offices in New York City. These must all be followed up. The National Library Board has its headquarters in New York City. This must be canvassed, as must the American Medical Society. It may be possible to have articles in those publications.

Some of the larger purchasers beside the jobbers must be approached. It is customary for sales to people such as Macy's to be made direct by the publisher.

On April first, when the book has been published, the decision will be reached by the stockholders as to the continuance of the office. If sales are going at a very rapid rate, there would be no question as to the necessity of the office.

There is naturally a question as to what would be done after April first if an office is not necessary. One of the usual printing services extended by book printers to publishers is that of shipping. The printer will attend to all details such as billing, collecting the money, and shipping for a publisher at cost. In other words, it is possible to turn over to a regular book printer all physical detail except writing, selling, and publicity.

A fact not generally realized is that book publishers do no printing. The printing, the art work, and all work attendant to issuing the book is done by specialized book printers. One of the duties of the management of the corporation will be attending to the printing details. Mr. Walsh of the John Day Printing Company recommended any one of the three printers competent to handle all details.

Another question is that of distribution and credit to book stores. There are only three book jobbers in the United States; any one of whom covers the entire country. Their credit is of the highest and they in turn take off the publishers hands all questions in regard to credit risks to the retail store. We have been told that we will have no trouble in securing any one of these three jobbers.

Taken all in all, there are plenty of details to be taken care of and sales promotional work to be done between the present time and April first.

SUBSCRIPTION

Date . . . .

On the basis of being a charter subscriber, I hereby subscribe for . . . . Twenty Five Dollar par value non-assessable shares of The One Hundred Men Corporation to be formed.

My check for . . . . is attached which is in full payment—partial payment. (cross out one)

In case this check is partial payment, I agree to pay an equal amount in thirty, sixty, ninety, and one hundred and twenty days from this date.

Signed _____

Street Address _____

City _____

State _____

CHECKS MAY BE MADE PAYABLE TO:
THE ALCOHOLIC FOUNDATION
or to—HENRY G. PARKHURST, Inc.

PLEASE MAIL TO:

HENRY G. PARKHURST, Inc.   WILLIAM J. RUDDELL
17 William Street   or   108 Harvey Street
Newark, New Jersey   Hackettstown, New Jersey

Hazelden Information and Educational Services is a division of the Hazelden Foundation, a not-for-profit organization. Since 1949, Hazelden has been a leader in promoting the dignity and treatment of people afflicted with the disease of chemical dependency.

The mission of the foundation is to improve the quality of life for individuals, families, and communities by providing a national continuum of information, education, and recovery services that are widely accessible; to advance the field through research and training; and to improve our quality and effectiveness through continuous improvement and innovation.

Stemming from that, the mission of this division is to provide quality information and support to people wherever they may be in their personal journey—from education and early intervention, through treatment and recovery, to personal and spiritual growth.

Although our treatment programs do not necessarily use everything Hazelden publishes, our bibliotherapeutic materials support our mission and the Twelve Step philosophy upon which it is based. We encourage your comments and feedback.

The headquarters of the Hazelden Foundation is in Center City, Minnesota. Additional treatment facilities are located in Chicago, Illinois; New York, New York; Plymouth, Minnesota; St. Paul, Minnesota; and West Palm Beach, Florida. At these sites, we provide a continuum of care for men and women of all ages. Our Plymouth facility is designed specifically for youth and families.

For more information on Hazelden, please call 1-800-257-7800. Or you may access our World Wide Web site on the Internet at **www.hazelden.org**.